NUNIVAK

KODIAK

KASKA

TLINGIT

SLAVEY

CHIPEWYAN

HAIDA

CARRIER

KUTENAI

NOOTKA

LAKE

PEND
D'OREILLE

ASSINIBOIN

ATSINA

CHINOOK

FLATHEAD

KAROK

MODOC

CHEYENNE

WINTU

MAIDU

ARAPAHO

SOUTHERN
UTE

JICARILL

NAVAJO

ACOMA

PIMA

NIHANCAN'S FEAST

OF BEAVER

NIHANCAN'S FEAST OF BEAVER

ANIMAL TALES OF THE NORTH AMERICAN INDIANS

Compiled and Edited by

EDWARD LAVITT AND ROBERT E. MCDOWELL

Illustrations by

BUNNY PIERCE HUFFMAN

Introduction by Linda J. Goodman

Maps by Deborah Reade

MUSEUM OF NEW MEXICO PRESS

10 9 8 7 6 5 4 3 2

Library of Congress Cataloging-in-Publication Data
Lavitt, Edward.
    Nihancan's feast of beaver: animal tales of the North American
 Indians   / Edward Lavitt and Robert E. McDowell.
      p. cm.
    Includes bibliographical references.
    ISBN 0-89013-210-0. — ISBN 0-89013-211-9 (pbk.)
    1. Indians of North America — Legends. 2. Animals — Folklore-
Juvenile literature. 3. Tales — North America. I. McDowell,
Robert E. (Robert Eugene), 1928-   II. Title.
E98.F5L35   1990
398.24'5293232 — dc20   90-42866
                                          CIP

Design by Jos. Trautwein.
Manufactured in the United States of America

Museum of New Mexico Press
P.O. Box 2087
Santa Fe, NM 87504-2087

ACKNOWLEDGMENTS

Grateful acknowledgment is made to the following for permission to reprint or adapt from previously published material. "Blue Jay's Theft of Dawn," from *California University Publications in American Archaeology and Ethnology*, v. 28, "Wintu Myths," by Cora DuBois and Dorothy Demetracopoulou, University of California Press, 1931. "Blood Clot," from *American Indian Myths and Legends*, by Richard Erdoes and Alfonso Ortiz, Pantheon Books, 1984. "The Flood," from *The Pollen Path*, by Margaret Schevill Link, Stanford University Press, 1956. "Fox Gets Back Her Fur," from *Pueblo Indian Folktales*, v. 49, by Aurelio M. Espinosa, Journal of American Folklore, 1936. "The Creation of the Earth," from *Mexican Border Ballads and Other Lore*, by Mody C. Boatwright, Texas Folklore Society, 1946. "Hare Slits His Nose While Visiting," from *Winnebago Hero Cycles: A Study in Aboriginal Literature*, by Paul Radin, Indiana University Publications in Anthropology and Linguistics, 1948. "How Coyote Got His Special Powers," from *Indian Legends of the Pacific Northwest*, by Ella E. Clark, University of California Press, 1969. "How the Seasons Came," from *The Assiniboines*, by James L. Long, University of Oklahoma Press, 1961. "Legend of the Roadrunner," from *Pima Indian Legends*, by Anna Shaw, University of Arizona Press, 1970. "Origin of Death and the Seasons," from *Myths of the Carrier Indians of British Columbia*, by Diamond Jenness, Journal of American Folklore, v. XVI, 1903. "The Race of the Turtle and the Beaver," from *Seneca Myths and Folktales*, by Arthur C. Parker, Buffalo Historical Society, 1923. "Readheaded Woodpecker and the Thunderbirds," from *Nootka Texts*, by Edward Sapir and Morris Swadesh, University of Pennsylvania / Linguistic Society of America, 1939. "The Seven Stars," from *Cheyenne Memories*, by John Stands in Timber, University of Nebraska Press, 1972.

 ABOUT THE AUTHORS

Edward Lavitt was for many years a teacher and counselor in schools in New York's Harlem and the South Bronx. The author of two previous books for children, he currently writes texts for the Literacy Volunteers of New York City.

For over twenty-five years Robert E. McDowell, Ph.D., worked at the University of Denver and the University of Texas, Arlington, teaching and writing about folklore and literatures of the Third World. The author of numerous books and articles, he lives on a farm in East Texas.

Contents

Introduction for the Adult Reader

Linda J. Goodman, Ph.D.

INTRODUCTION FOR THE ADULT READER

Linda J. Goodman, Ph.D., Ethnohistorian, Museum of New Mexico

"He opened the basket and light flew out." Thus ends a California Wintu tale about the origin of light, a natural element crucial to the survival of all living things on earth. The natural environment plays a key role in the lives of Native American people and also in their myths and stories. Traditionally, American Indians have lived off the land and have come to know it and its inhabitants intimately; survival depended on this knowledge. The great love and respect held for nature also is clearly evident in the stories told by the elders to the children.

Every tribe has its own origin tales — how the earth, living things, and supernaturals came to be. Non-Indians also have a story concerning the origin of Indian people, and it is quite different from some of those collected in this book. According to anthropologists, humans have inhabited the North American continent for only a very short time. Approximately twenty to thirty thousand years ago, geologists theorize, a land bridge across the Bering Strait connected Siberia (the Old World) with Alaska (the New World). The first people who crossed it came as hunters and gatherers who wandered into this new area while seeking food. As the years passed, small groups migrated to different parts of the Western Hemisphere and selected particular territories as theirs. Those who arrived later either had to push out earlier inhabitants or move further in order to find unoccupied land in which to make their homes. Thus, very slowly, the land became home to many different groups of people, who are known today as Native Americans.

Great diversity exists among American Indian Tribes. According to anthropologist Harold Driver, approximately two thousand separate languages were spoken by Indian peoples at the time of initial European contact in 1492. Since more than one tribe often spoke the same language, it is probable that well over two thousand tribes inhabited the land. Even though today the total number of tribes is fewer and a number of the languages have become extinct, still many continue to be spoken and Indian children are learning them from their elders. According to linguists Campbell and Mithuen, the many North American Indian languages have been grouped into sixty-two families. Each family of languages may include from one to more than a dozen separate languages within it. (This would parallel the European Romance Language Family which includes the separate languages of Italian, French, and Spanish.) In total, approximately three to four hundred separate Indian languages still exist on the North American continent.

Given the complexity of the tribal situation in North America, anthropologists have created "culture areas" in order more easily to discuss particular groups of tribes who share certain (though not all) characteristics. Tribes included in a culture area live in one geographic locality, share a similar climate and natural environment, and usually have one or more of the following culture traits in common: house types; food production; clothing types; ceremonial and religious organization; social, economic, and political organization.

North America has been subdivided by some experts into nine culture areas, each with its own climate and environment (see maps for location of each culture, as well as tribal, area). Each area includes a great many tribes which are different in some ways but share other features in common. The nine culture areas featured in this book include the Plains, Basin-Plateau, California, Northwest Pacific Coast, Eskimo, Sub-Arctic, Eastern Woodland, Southeastern, and Southwestern areas.

The tales included in this collection are drawn from each of the above nine culture areas. One tale was selected from each of four tribes located within a particular culture area. In these tales children can learn about the behaviors and actions of humans, animals, and the supernaturals who inhabit their world. In Indian cultures, all life is considered valuable and sacred and is a part of the powerful spiritual forces of nature. Therefore, all living things are treated with respect and honor, the bad as well as the good. Bad examples are just as necessary as good ones in order to teach about the full range of life; therefore they are included here.

The Importance of Storytelling in Indian Cultures

First and foremost, storytelling is a delightful educational form by means of which Indian elders teach basic cultural principles, moral values, and proper ways of behaving to the younger generation. Although the tales are entertaining, this is not their primary purpose. It is to teach how to live a good life among one's own people. Living properly involves learning where one fits and the expectations of one's society. It is also most important to learn to live in harmony with both the natural environment and with the people around one. Stories provide examples of how to do this.

Many, though not all, characters in these stories are animals, who play important parts in the myths and tales of most Indian peoples. These creatures, found in the natural environment, often have human characteristics as well as magical and super-

natural abilities. They usually speak and act as humans do and sometimes change from animal to human form (by taking off their skins) and then change back to animal form again (by putting their skins back on). When necessary, they will just change shape without warning, as in the Chipewyan tale "White Bear and Black Bear." Here, Crow, a trickster character, changes himself into a baby in order to retrieve the Sun for all the animals after it had been stolen and hidden away by White Bear.

An animal with the same name can have very different characteristics in different Indian tribes. Spider, for example, can be a source of good things in one culture and can be evil in another culture. In the Southwest, Spider Grandmother is very wise and helpful to Navajo people and teaches them many things. However, among the Atsina (Gros Ventre) tribe, the spider is a cunning, crafty character who kills people and is capable of other bad deeds, as seen in the tale "Spider's Revenge." Among the Nunivak Eskimo, the spider woman kills to get her way in the story "Spider Comes to Earth," but then appears to reform and become a better character. She becomes responsible and cares for her family properly. So, it is clear that the same animal can provide quite different lessons in cultural values.

In the present collection of tales, some animals provide positive role models, while others provide negative ones. The good characters live well and fit happily into their surroundings. The Maidu Tale "Earth Namer and the Creation," is one example. Earth Namer, who is the Creator, Turtle, and Coyote all behave properly; thus things are created as they should be and all is right with the world.

On the other hand, other characters break the rules at times and make life difficult for themselves and others. The Southeast Greenland Eskimo story, "When the Ravens Could Speak," tells in very succinct form what can happen to someone who uses words of abuse and who lies and is ill-tempered.

Many of these stories have a definite moral, as in the Nootka tale, "Redheaded Woodpecker and the Thunderbirds," where the Thunderbirds are punished for stealing Woodpecker's wife. Not every story paints a pretty picture, nor are all the characters honorable. Some of them behave despicably and in this way present examples of how one should not act or be. The trickster spider in the Atsina story, "Spider's Revenge," is one example of an unpleasant character who kills a bear and is unkind to other creatures. They then treat him badly in return. These are behaviors that children should not emulate.

On the other hand, animals sometimes sacrifice their lives so that the lives of men can be better, as in the Assiniboin tale "How the Seasons Came." Five outstanding animals died while bringing Summer to the Assiniboin people. In another case, Coyote stole fire for the Karok people and then had all the animals help him get it to those who needed it, in the tale "The Origin of Fire." Thus animals can be helpful and can be protectors of humans.

Some stories indicate that life is harsh and not always kind and pleasant, as in the Modoc tale "The Great Spirit and the Grizzlies," where the grizzlies protected and raised the Great Spirit's youngest daughter after she was blown away in a severe storm. The Great Spirit, being angry because his daughter was kept from him for so many years, killed the mother grizzly and made the rest of the grizzlies go around on four paws like all the other animals, even though they had kept his daughter alive and she had been happy living with them.

Creation stories of many varieties are quite common in American Indian tribes and include such themes as the creation of the land, the animals, people, plants, sun, moon, stars, fire, and so forth.

Frequently there is a supernatural power, the Great Creator, who is assisted by helpful animal creatures. The Maidu story "Earth Namer and the Creation," presents a fine example. The Jicarilla tale, "The Origin of Fire," tells how Coyote helped bring fire to this group of Apaches.

A related theme might be called "How things came to be as they are." In these tales, certain characters act in certain ways, often they misbehave, and then something happens to them that teaches them the lesson they need to learn. In the Passamaquoddy tale "The Partridge's Wife," the wife investigates something that belongs to her husband and which is not her business. By doing this, she causes evil to enter and kill her husband's brother. To escape her husband's anger she throws herself into the river and becomes a sheldrake duck. This duck now has red on its feet and feathers because her hands were so stained when she was investigating the secret hiding place of her husband's brother. Ever since, the sheldrake duck has had these red stains. A number of other stories of this type are included in this collection.

Great floods and the killing of monsters are two other themes which occur in Indian stories. The Kutenai tale "The Great Monster and the Great Flood" incorporates both in one story, while the Flathead tale, "Coyote Kills a Giant," has Coyote outwitting a giant in order to kill him and make the land safe for everyone.

Two special kinds of characters appear in a number of these stories: the culture hero and the trickster. The culture hero breathes life into people and animals, creates their world, and often teaches them what they need to know in both their daily life and ceremonial life. The culture hero is endowed with supernatural powers, performs wonderful magic feats for his/her people, has a series of adventures, sometimes rids the people of enemies, gives them certain foods, and teaches them various occupations and ceremonies.

The trickster is the character who breaks the rules and rebels against authority. He plays tricks and pranks on those who are unsuspecting and is cunning and clever at cheating and destroying his enemy. At times he will change his shape (become another character) in order to get his way. Frequently he is paid back for misbehaving and loses what he sought to win. Often the adventures of trickster make people laugh because they know he has misbehaved and will be punished somehow for going against society. "There he goes again," they will say. Coyote is perhaps the best known trickster in many American Indian tribes, and several tales concerning him are included.

Indian tales do not necessarily fit the format of European tales where all parts logically follow each other and have clear endings. At times these tales may seem inconsistent to non-Indians. For example, in some stories the culture hero may also be a trickster, and this may be a source of confusion. In the Arapaho tale, "Nihancan's Feast of Beaver," Nihancan, the culture hero, is the creator of all things, yet we see him killing the beavers to make a meal for himself. When he engages in this behavior he has become the trickster, cunning and deceitful. However, he still acts as the Creator in that he leaves one male and one female beaver alive and tells them to return to their den and increase. The same character can thus be both hero and trickster, as is sometimes the case with humans.

For Arapaho children this story provides lessons in death, and teaches them what happens when one acts in unacceptable ways. The importance of the creator for all life and the cunning of both Nihancan and Coyote are revealed in the process. Even the Creator, when he acted as a trickster and killed most of the beavers, was punished for his action. He was not allowed to eat the meal which he had prepared. Instead, Coyote, another trick-ster, outwitted him, ate all Nihancan's food, and thus punished him. One learns that it does not pay to behave as Nihancan or Coyote behave. Finally, Nihancan punished Coyote by burning the hair on his legs, because he was greedy and would not share the beaver meat. Thus, both characters had misbehaved and each punished the other. In the meantime, the remaining beavers had survived and would create a new family.

The characters who are the actors in the stories presented in this collection teach children how to live in their societies. By their examples children learn how to hunt, sing, dance, perform ceremonies, make houses and clothing, be good people, and seek the supernatural power that will guide them throughout their lives.

These characters also help give children a sense of identity. The animals, the humans, and the supernaturals each have a particular place in the world and know how to act. The children learn this about the characters and also about themselves. Essential ideas and values are presented in an easily understood and treasured form. The same stories provide refreshers for the adults who tell the stories or listen while others are telling them. One is never too old to hear these tales.

Perhaps one Navajo storyteller stated a common Indian point of view most clearly:

It's too easy to become sick, because there are always things happening to confuse our minds. We need to have ways of thinking, of keeping things stable, healthy, beautiful. We try for a long life, but lots of things can happen to us. So. . .we keep our lives in order with the stories. We have to relate our lives to the stars and the sun, the animals, and to all of nature or else we will go crazy or get sick. [*]

[*]Toelken, Barre. The Dynamics of Folklore. Boston: Houghton Mifflin Co., 1979: 96.

PLAINS CULTURE AREA

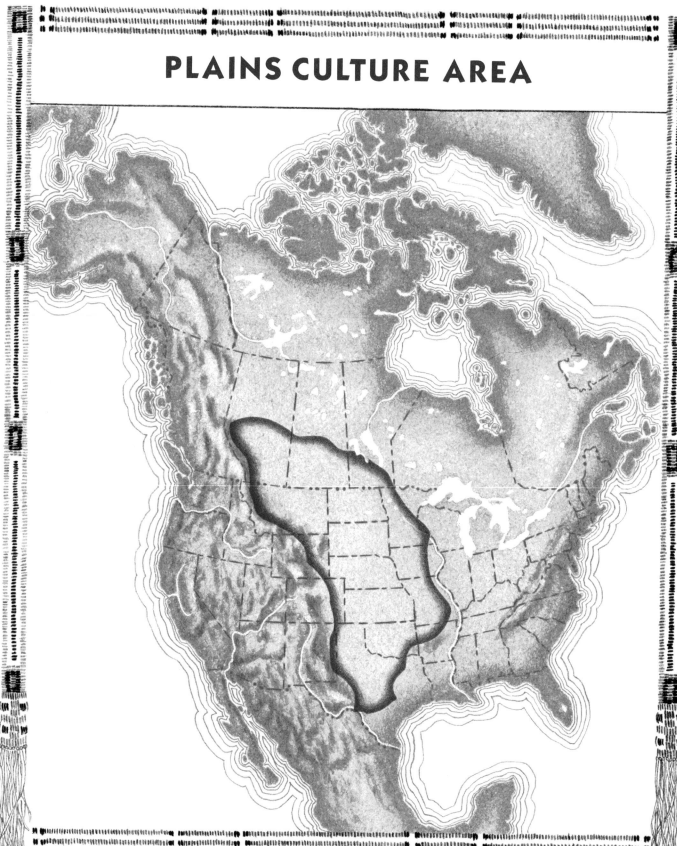

The Plains culture area includes the tribes who live between the Mississippi River on the East and the Rocky Mountains on the west, the Saskatchewan River Basin in Canada on the north and central Texas on the south. In this vast expanse of land many of the people lived in circular lodges covered with earth, grass, skins, or mats, in semi-permanent farming  villages. They did some hunting and gathering on foot. After they acquired the horse from the Spanish in the 1500s, they became great buffalo hunters and warriors and adopted a more nomadic way of life which seldom included agriculture. They lived in skin tepees and made hide clothing. Religion centered around the seeking of a personal spirit helper through a sacred vision.  Many tribes held an annual Sun Dance Ceremony where men made vows to participate and sacrifice if they received certain  supernatural assistance.

ARAPAHO

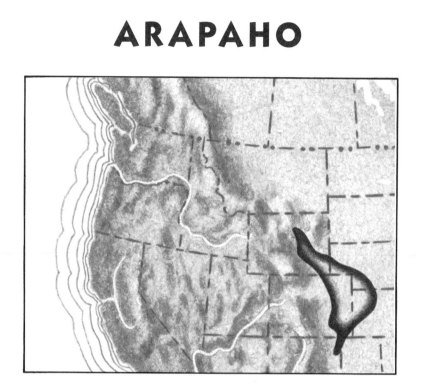

In some of the Arapaho myths, Nihancan was the
Creator who fashioned all things from some earth scraped from the feet of a
diving duck. This was when everything was water.
In this tale, Nihancan is supposed to have human
form. He is sometimes a trickster who
will try to get his way by being clever and sly. The
story shows Nihancan getting even with Coyote, one of the most popular
trickster characters found in American Indian tales.

NIHANCAN'S FEAST OF BEAVER

One day, Nihancan went down the river and came to several lakes in which there were plenty of beavers. "Well! You folks are starving yourselves here; there are several lakes just over the hill where there are plenty of nice clean young cottonwood trees and yellow willows on the banks; the water is very deep and green. You ought to go over there and live upon the fine trees and drink that good water. I will show you the way and will take you over," said Nihancan. "All right! He is advising us for our benefit," said the beavers.

Nihancan cut a big stick for a club, and the beavers got out of their dens and started off over the land. Nihancan followed them. When they had gone a distance, Nihancan said to the little beaver who was behind, "This is what I am going to kill you with," showing the club stick. The little beaver ran up to his father and mother and told them what Nihancan had said. The beavers stopped. "Nihancan, this little beaver says that you showed him the stick that you were going to kill him with! How is that?" said the father of the little beaver.

"Well, no, I didn't say any such thing. I told him that when you get over the other side of the hill, you will have this kind of food; perhaps it will be tastier and more tender. I was showing him the kind of wood that grows there," said Nihancan.

When the beavers had gone a little farther from their dam, Nihancan struck one dead. The others turned and began running back to the dam, Nihancan running after them and knocking them down

until there were only two left, a male and a female. "You go back to your den so that you may increase in number and kind," said Nihancan.

Nihancan then gathered up all the dead beavers, made a pit in which he placed them, covered them up with dirt, and built a fire to roast them. "That is the way I get my food," said Nihancan.

Now there were two cottonwood trees standing nearby, and the wind was blowing hard so that the branches were waving. There were two limbs on the top of the tree rubbing together and making a squeaking noise. "Oh! Stop fighting," said Nihancan. When he saw that he could not stop them from fighting, he climbed the tree to part them, and taking hold of each limb, he became stuck between them. While Nihancan was fastened between the limbs up in the tree, Coyote came running up and dug out the roasted meat. "Say, partner, don't eat them all!" said Nihancan. But Coyote ate them all and ran away.

After he had freed himself, Nihancan trailed Coyote and found him asleep in the grass, pretty well stuffed with beaver meat. Nihancan went to the windward side of Coyote and built a fire so close to him that it burned the hair off his legs and awakened him.

"You are punished because you are so greedy," said Nihancan. "From now on, you will have yellow fur around your legs so that everyone will know who you are," said Nihancan as he ran off chuckling to himself.

ASSINIBOIN

When they were first created, according to their

legends, the Plains tribe called Assiniboin had only the season of winter.

When some of the people discovered that

there was a place where summer was kept, a party of animals

was sent to get it. This story tells how the animals bring

the rest of the seasons to the Assiniboin.

HOW THE SEASONS CAME

A long time ago, the Assiniboin people lived in country almost always covered with snow. There were no horses and only dogs were used to carry things.

A small war party that had been gone a long time returned and went at once to the chief's lodge. They told him to call his councilors together because they had an important message. The chief set food before them and sent his camp crier to call the council members to his lodge.

The spokesman said, "We have been away from our people for many moons. We have set foot on land that belongs to others; we have set foot on land without snow. It is in the direction of where the sun rests at midday.

"In the middle of a large encampment there is a lodge painted yellow. In this the summer is kept in a bag hung on a tripod. Four old men guard it day and night. One sits in the back, directly under the tripod; another lies across the entrance; and two others sit on each side of the fireplace."

The chief and his headmen sat in council until one of them said, "Let us call in a representative of each kind of the fast-running animals and ask them to help us bring this wonderful thing to our country." So the camp crier went forth and called to those medicine men who had fast-running animals for their helpers to invite them to the lodge.

When all were in council, the chief said, "My people and my brothers [the animals], far in the direction of midday there is the summer, and I call you here to make plans to bring it to our people. The ones who go will never come back alive, but they will do a great good to our people and their kind, for their children will enjoy the breath of the summer forever."

It was decided to send the Lynx, the Red Fox, the Antelope, the Coyote, and the Wolf. The young warriors who knew the way were to guide the runners to the encampment.

After many days' march, they arrived near the camp and took council. The spokesman said, "The Lynx will go into the lodge and bring out the bag containing the summer because nobody can hear him walk. He will give it to the Red Fox, who will be waiting for him along the way. From there, the Antelope will carry it to the Coyote, who will take it to the Wolf, who is long-winded, and he will bring it to us by the big river where we will be waiting. From there, we will take it to our people."

So the Lynx was left there and the rest went back in the direction from which they had come.

The Red Fox first was told to take his position, and so on until all the animals were stationed a certain distance apart according to the ability of the runner. If an animal were short-winded, it was not required to make a long run for the bag was to be carried at the fastest speed.

Toward morning, before the light showed and when slumber was in every lodge, the Lynx softly walked to the yellow lodge and looked in. The four old men were all asleep. The bag containing the summer was hanging on the tripod in the back part of the lodge.

The summer was in the form of spring water. It moved about in a bag made from the stomach of a buffalo. Now and then it overflowed and trickled along the ground, under the tripod, and in its wake green grass and many different kinds of plants and flowers grew luxuriantly.

Cautiously, on stealthy feet, the Lynx entered, stepping over the entrance, and, with a quick jerk, snapped the cord that held the bag. Seizing it tightly in his teeth, he plunged through the door and sped away.

Almost the same instant, the old men awakened and gave the alarm: "The summer has been stolen!" The cry went from lodge to lodge, and in a short time, a group on fast horses was after the Lynx.

They were fast gaining on the Lynx when he gave the bag to the Red Fox, who was waiting. The horsemen then killed the Lynx and started after the Fox, who, after a time, gave the bag to the Antelope. The Antelope took it to the Coyote, who brought it to the Wolf, the long-winded one, who was to deliver it to the waiting party. Each time the bag was passed to the next runner, the winded animal was killed by the pursuers.

The fast horses were tired but gained steadily on the Wolf. As he sped across the country, the snow melted directly behind him, the grass sprang up green, and trees and bushes unfolded their leaves as the summer passed by. Fowls seemed to join the pursuit as flock after flock flew northward.

As the Wolf crossed the river, the ice moved and broke up. By the time the horsemen reached it, the river was flowing and the banks were full of ice. This halted the Southern people. In sign language they said to the Assiniboin, "Let us bargain with each other for the possession of the summer." After a time, it was decided that each would keep the summer for six moons. Then it was to be taken back to the river and delivered to the waiting party.

That agreement was kept so there was summer half of the year in each country. In that way, there were the two seasons, the winter and the summer.

After many two-seasons had passed, the head men of the Assiniboin decided to have the cranes carry the summer back and forth. They were always the first of the migratory fowl to go south. They moved by easy stages, stopping for long periods at good feeding grounds. By that method of carrying the summer, the winter gradually followed the cranes so that, instead of the sudden winter as when the summer was taken south by the men, the fall season, *Pdanyedu,* made its appearance. Long before the cranes returned, there were signs among the plants and animals that the summer was on its way north. That time was called *Wedu,* the spring.

A late fall or spring was a sign that the cranes had found good feeding grounds and waited there too long. An early winter or summer was a sign that the carriers had winged their way south or north in haste.

As the cranes flew over an encampment, they always circled several times and, with their loud calls, seemed to announce their arrival or departure.

So, finally, the Assiniboin had four seasons: the winter, *Waniyedu;* the summer, *Mnogedu;* the fall, *Pdanyedu;* and the spring, *Wedu.*

CHEYENNE

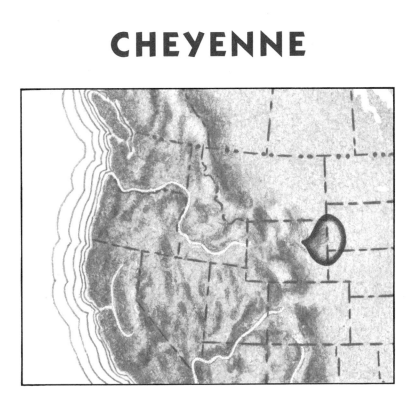

"John Stands in Timber" was the name of one of the

historians of the Cheyenne people. He wrote about the old storytellers who

retold stories that they had heard from their

elders. Before telling each tale, a storyteller would go through a

ritual that involved touching the ground with his

hands and rubbing his hands over his head and body.

The storyteller would repeat this again.

According to John Stands in Timber, the ritual

meant that the Creator had made the earth and human beings

and that the Creator was present in the telling of the

tale that followed.

THE SEVEN STARS

One time, long ago, a man, a wife, and their only child, a beautiful girl, lived in a big village in a valley. When the girl was old enough, her mother began teaching her how to use porcupine quills, sewing them onto deerskin clothing and blankets in lovely designs. The girl became good at this; her work was among the finest done by all the people.

One day, she began to work on an outfit of buckskin clothing for a man, decorating it with her best designs in dyed quills. It took her a month to finish it, and when she was done, she started on another, and that took a month also. She kept on until she had finished seven outfits in the same way.

When the work was completed, she told her mother and father, "There are seven young men who are brothers who live a long journey from here. Since I have no brothers or sisters of my own, I am going out to find them and take them for my brothers and live with them. Someday they will be known to all the people on earth." Her parents did not try to stop her.

The next morning, her mother helped the girl make two bags to pack the clothing in. They put three of the outfits in each of these, packed them on two dogs, and the girl herself carried the smallest outfit.

The girl traveled a long distance with the two dogs until she came to a wide river with a large tepee on its bank. As she approached the tepee, a little boy came running out, saying, "I am the young-est of the seven brothers. The rest are hunting and will be back by sundown."

The girl said, "I came to find you all. I am going to take you for my brothers."

They led the dogs to the tepee and unloaded the packs. Then the girl spoke to the dogs and turned them loose, and they ran off, going home. Next, she unwrapped the smallest buckskin outfit and gave it to the boy, saying, "My brother, this is a gift from me." He immediately put on his new moccasins, leggings, shirt, and little blanket and he was happy because of their beautiful designs.

Inside the tepee, the little boy pointed to each of the beds in turn, indicating to which of the brothers it belonged; on each, she put one of the buckskin outfits. Then she prepared a meal and waited for them to return.

At sundown, they approached the camp, and the youngest ran out to meet them, throwing himself on the ground and kicking his legs up in the air so they would be sure to see his new moccasins and leggings.

"Where did you get those things?" they asked.

"You said not to let anyone near the tepee," he said, "but a girl came, and before I could tell her to stay out, she said she had brought us all some new clothes, and she is taking us for brothers. She is a beautiful girl." They were pleased with the news and went into the tepee.

In those days, brothers and sisters did not talk to one another, but since the smallest had already spoken to the girl, he kept on. Acting as interpreter, he told the girl what the others wanted and gave her their answers. They lived together and were happy to have someone prepare their meals.

One morning, when the older brothers were out hunting, a yellow buffalo calf came running up to the tepee and stopped a little distance from it, looking all around.

"Buffalo Calf," said the little boy, "what do you want?"

"I was sent by the buffalo," the calf answered. "They want your sister, and I am to take her back with me."

"No, you can't have her," said the boy. "The other brothers are hunting, and you must wait until they come back."

The calf ran away, kicking and jumping until he was out of sight. In a little while, a two-year-old heifer came running up the same way and stopped outside the tepee.

"Two-Year-Old Heifer," said the little boy, "what do you want?"

"I was sent by the buffalo," she answered. "They want your sister, and I will take her back with me. If you don't let her go, Buffalo Cow is coming."

"No," said the little boy. "Go back and tell them they cannot have her."

Two-Year-Old Heifer ran away like the calf, kicking and jumping until she was out of sight. In a little while, a third buffalo came—a big cow.

"Buffalo Cow," said the little boy, "what do you want? Why are you bothering us?"

"I was sent by the buffalo," said the cow. "They want your sister. If you don't let her go, the herd is coming here after her, and you will all be killed."

"Well, you cannot have her," said the little boy. "Go back and tell them." Buffalo Cow ran away, kicking and jumping like the others.

Soon the brothers returned from hunting, and when the little boy told them what had happened, they were afraid. Before long, they heard a noise like the earth shaking and saw a great herd of buffalo coming toward the tepee with a big bull in the lead.

"Hurry," cried one of the six brothers to the youngest. "You have power that can keep anything from touching you. Use it and save us!"

The little boy ran and got his bow and arrows. He aimed into the top of a nearby tree, and when the arrow hit it, the tree began to grow until the top was almost out of sight. The brothers lifted the girl into the lowest branches and climbed after her, and in a minute, the ground below them was covered with buffalo. All they could hear was snorting and bawling.

Then the lead bull came forward and started to circle the tree trunk down below. He was angry, shaking his head and pawing the ground. Soon he charged at the tree and stopped just short of it. He did this three times, but the fourth time, he struck it and cut a big piece out of it with his horns.

Four times he did the same thing: charging and stopping three times and then gouging out big chunks of the trunk on the fourth charge. The fourth time, it swayed and then began to topple and fall.

"Hurry!" cried the brothers to the boy. "Save us!"

Quickly, he aimed and shot another arrow far into the sky. It vanished from sight, and they felt the tree growing upward after it. At last it hit the sky. They all climbed out of the branches and stayed there, turned into stars.

They can still be seen at night as the Seven Stars, called by some the Big Dipper.

ATSINA

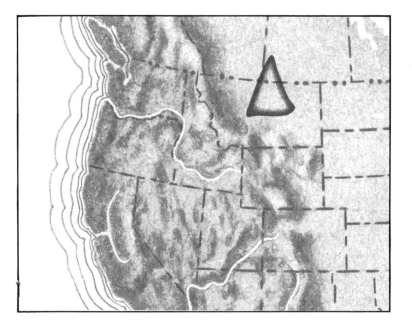

The Atsina were buffalo hunters who often

decorated their clothing and bags with bright quills and with painted colored

designs. The tepees of Atsina warriors were

ornamented with paintings that showed their war

records and rank.

One of the most important deities of the

Atsina was Nihaat, whose name means "Spider."

Nihaat could perform magic, and he often had ridiculous adventures as he

traveled about. In this Atsina tale, Spider

works his magic to get his revenge on Stone, who had played a

trick on him.

SPIDER'S REVENGE

Spider, being a restless fellow, could never stay in one place for very long but was continually making little excursions about the country. One day, as he was walking down the riverbank, he saw Bear on the opposite side and, wishing to have some fun with him, shouted across, "Ho, Bear!" Bear raised himself and looked all around.

"How ridiculous you are!" called Spider. "Your eyes are small and squinty, and the hair is dark around them!"

At this, Bear became very angry and, splashing into the river, swam across to punish his tormentor; but Spider, fearing Bear's wrath, ran away quickly. The infuriated animal pursued, and Spider, seeing him come on with bristling hair and open mouth, was much alarmed and, as he ran, tried to think of a way to escape. As he was speeding along, he came to a large pile of Stones and, stopping, said to them, "Brothers, let us make a sweat lodge here."

The lodge appeared as he spoke, and some of the Stones piled themselves around the edge of the cover while a few went inside. The jester entered, and soon Bear came up looking very angry. Spider put his head out and called to him:

"Brother, what is wrong? Whom are you chasing? I saw that imp Spider running by and tried to stop him, but he seemed to be in a hurry and went on. No doubt he has been up to some mischief! Anyway, there is no use running yourself to death, and you had better take a sweat, for you might get sick, being so overheated. You go in first while I stay outside and open the lodge for you when you have finished."

Bear agreed and went in. Spider pulled the flap down, whispering to the Stones, "Brothers, sit on this flap and do not let him get out!"

In the meantime, Bear had been pouring water on the heated stones inside and the steam was getting very hot, so that he soon had enough and cried, "Brother, open the door!"

Spider's response was to whisper to the Stones, "Hold fast, brothers! Don't let him out!" Swinging a club in his hand, Spider walked watchfully around the lodge, and every time the sweater's head showed against the cover, he dealt him a blow until, at length, Bear was dead.

"Now I shall have a feast," chuckled Spider, and he began to skin his victim.

As he busily cut and slashed, Coyote joined him and said, "Brother, give the entrails to me; I am very hungry!"

But the other answered impatiently, "Leave me alone! You are always interfering!"

The beggar persisted until at last he was told to take a portion of the entrails to the river and wash them, and for doing that he was to have some for himself. Coyote went to the river, but instead of washing the entrails, he ate them and came back with a sorrowful story of how Fish had snatched them from his paws. Spider gave him the rest, advising him to use more care, and as soon as Coyote was out of sight, he followed, for he suspected that he was being deceived. Creeping up to the bank, he saw the thief devouring the tripe, and without a word, he ran back to the camp where he awaited the deceiver.

Soon Coyote appeared, whining, "Fish robbed me again!"

But Spider, with a large stone in his hand, exclaimed, "Robbed you again, did they?" and knocked him down. After a while, Coyote regained his senses, and his assailant, feeling remorseful, fed him and told him to go to their grandmother and borrow her cooking pot. Coyote went out to a patch of brush and shouted:

"Grandmother, we want to use your cooking pot!" Soon the vessel came rolling down, out of the bushes, and Spider commanded it to fill itself with water and sit on the fire, all of which the magic utensil did. Spider now finished cutting up the bear and, placing the flesh in the receptacle, stirred up a hot fire. When the meat was cooked, he spread it out on the grass and shouted, "Spider is inviting everything that lives to come and eat with him!" and all the creatures came and swarmed around him. He told them to sit in rows and seated himself on a nearby Stone with Coyote beside him. "I am going to eat first, and after that, I shall feed all of you," the feast-giver explained. He started to get up to reach for the food but he was stuck to his seat and could not move.

"Brother," he said to Stone, "don't do that; don't hold me." It only answered, "No, I always stay in one place for four years."

Not knowing that Coyote had told Stone to play the trick, Spider appealed to him to move the meat closer. When Coyote knew that Spider could not rise, he cried, "All you animals seize the meat and eat it quickly! Our brother is stuck to his seat and cannot get away!"

The animals fell upon the food, and soon it had disappeared despite Spider's piteous pleading that a little should be left for him. Then, mocking and laughing at him, they left him alone and the Stone released him. Here and there, at the edge of the fire, he gathered up the little fragments they had overlooked, intending to make a meal from them, when a spark flew out and struck his bare belly, burning him so badly that he jumped back, spilling the scraps in the fire. This aggravated his ill-temper, and, remembering the trick played on him by Stone, he called the dry Sticks scattered around:

"Brothers, come into the fire!" They all came and threw themselves on it. Stone viewed the preparation with alarm.

"Let me go!" he begged, but Spider only answered, "Let us see if you will remain in one place for four years!" He placed it in the fire, sitting on it to hold it securely, and Stone soon crumbled into pieces; Spider himself was somewhat scorched, but he did not mind that, having had his revenge.

"Brother," he said, "hereafter, when anyone puts you into a fire, you will break." And this is the reason stones break in the fire.

BASIN-PLATEAU CULTURE AREA

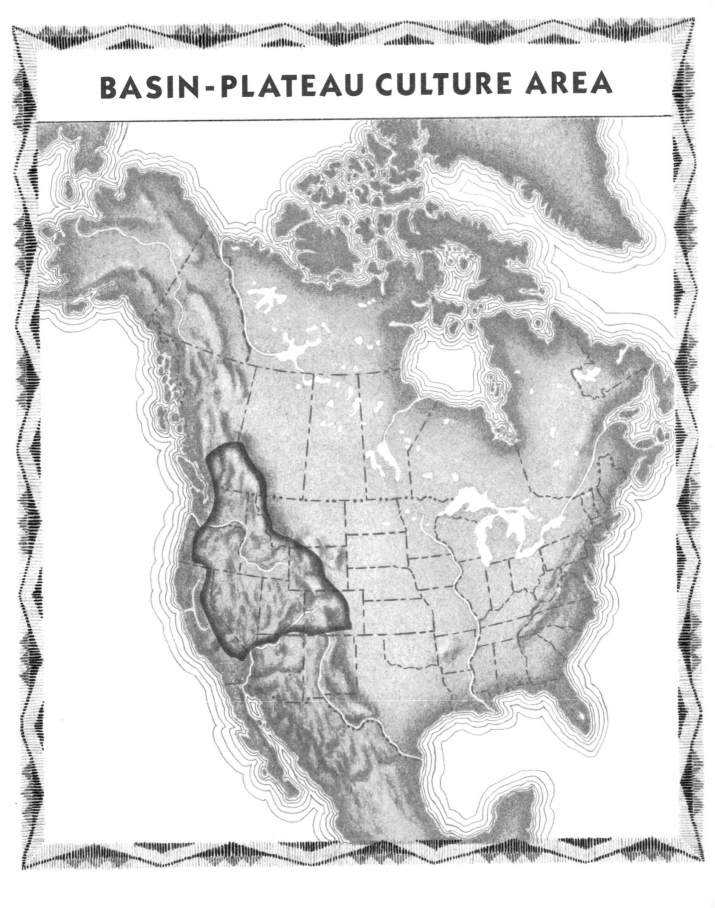

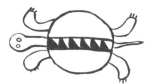 The Basin-Plateau culture area extended from the Rocky Mountains on the east to the Sierra Nevada and Cascade Mountains on the west, and from Central British Columbia on the north to the Utah-  Arizona border on the south. The people survived by hunting and gathering throughout this region and by fishing for salmon in the northern areas. Shelters were made of juniper or willow pole frames covered with brush, bark strips, or woven reed or grass mats. They also made brush wickiups. None of these people practiced agricul- ture. Religion involved shamans responsible for curing illness in the Basin area, while in the  Plateau, people acquired guardian spirits by going on a vision quest. The latter were also involved in annual Win- ter Spirit Dancing Ceremonies.

SOUTHERN UTE

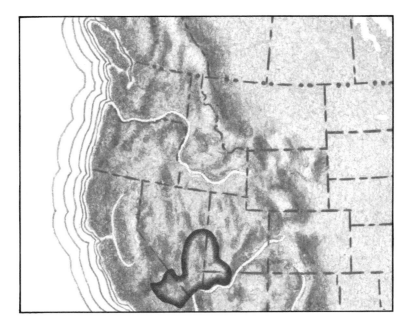

This creation story from the Southern Ute tells of
the mighty power of the Buffalo tribe.

BLOOD CLOT

Long ago a very old man and his wife lived alone and hunted for game, but it was scarce and they were hungry. One day the man discovered some buffalo tracks and followed them to the place where the animal had stopped. There he found only a big clot of blood, which he wrapped in his shirt and carried home.

The old man told his wife to boil the blood, and she put it into the kettle with water from the creek. But before it came to a boil over the fire, they heard cries inside the kettle. The man ran up to it and pulled out a baby, a little boy, who had somehow formed out of the blood clot.

The old couple washed the baby and wrapped him up. By the next morning he had grown much larger, and that day he continued to grow until he could crawl about by himself. The second day he was able to walk a little; by the third day he was walking with ease. The couple called him Blood Clot and came to treat him as their son.

The old man made little arrows so that the child could learn to shoot. Soon Blood Clot needed larger arrows, and with them he began to hunt birds and other small game. He never brought the game home himself, but sent the old man for it. One day Blood Clot returned from hunting and said, "I have killed something with a striped back." The man went out and fetched an animal a little bigger than a mouse, which he cooked for the three of them. The next day the boy announced, "I have killed a white short-tailed animal." It was a cottontail, which the man also cooked.

The day after that, Blood Clot went farther and killed a badger. "I have killed an animal in a hole in the ground," he said, and the man brought the creature home and cooked it. The following day when the boy returned, he said, "I have killed an animal with black ears and a black tail." To the old man's joy, it was a female deer. The three of them ate and were happy.

Next Blood Clot said, "I have killed a big fellow with big antlers." It was an elk, so again the family feasted on meat. The old man gave the boy a full-sized bow and arrows, and Blood Clot went into the mountains and shot a mountain goat. "I have killed a big fellow with big horns in the mountains," he said when he came down. "Every day," the old man said proudly, "he kills a different kind of animal."

Now their troubles were over, and they had an easy time. Blood Clot killed a mountain lion. Then he tracked and shot an otter: "I have killed an animal with nice fur, living in the water." The old man tanned the skin to make strings for tying the boy's braids. The following day Blood Clot found a beaver: "I have killed a water animal with a tail of this size."

At last there came a day when Blood Clot said, "I want to visit the village where many people live. Before that, I will go on my last hunt for you, all day and all night. First I want you to tie up the tent, put rocks on the edge, and fasten the door lest the night wind carry it away. Though the wind will be strong, don't go outdoors and don't be afraid. I will call when you can come out."

The old couple obeyed, and he hunted all night while they were sleeping. About daybreak they heard a big noise, forerunner of a wind that threatened to tip over the tent. The man was frightened and wanted to go out, but the wife held him back, reminding him of what their son had said.

When daylight came, they heard their son's voice: "Come on out; I'll show you something." They unfastened the door and saw dead buffalo lying all around.

"I have done this for you," Blood Clot said. "Dry the meat and hides; save the meat and it will last you for a long time." The young man asked his mother to fix him a lunch, and she gave him pemmican. "Now my parents have plenty of food," he said. As he left, they cried and asked him to return.

Wearing buckskin leggings, carrying a quiver of mountain lion skin, Blood Clot began to travel. After a few days he reached the village. At the outskirts he asked for the chief's house, and a man told him, "It is in the center." There he found the chief with his wife and daughter. They invited him to sit down, and the chief asked him where he came from and what his tribe was.

"I don't know what tribe I belong to. I have come to visit you," Blood Clot replied. The chief stepped outdoors and shouted to the people to come and meet their visitor. The villagers were starving for lack of game, but all gathered at the chief's house and sat down.

The chief said, "Do any of you know the tribe of this young man?" People named the tribes—Deer, Elk, Otters, Beavers, and others. They asked him whether he belonged to any of these, but he thought not. At last one old man said, "I think I know from the power in him, although I may be mistaken. I think he is one of the Buffalo." Blood Clot thought about it, and finally agreed.

The people of the village asked Blood Clot to stay and marry the chief's daughter. He agreed to this as well, and the wedding was held.

That evening he asked his father-in-law to bring one arrow from the tipi. When the chief returned, Blood Clot told him to have all the tipis fastened and to warn the people that they should stay indoors, for there would be a great storm. The chief told the villagers, and at daybreak when they heard a big noise, they cried out in fear but did not leave their tipis.

Then Blood Clot called to the chief, who came out to find dead buffalo before every lodge. At his son-in-law's bidding he summoned the whole village for a feast, and all were happy.

Blood Clot stayed there until one day when a group of villagers went out to hunt buffalo. Long before this, he had told his wife, "You know the Buffalo Calf? I am part of that, it is part of me, so you must never say the word 'calf.'" When the party killed some buffalo and were butchering, another herd came running past. His wife pointed and called, "Kill that calf!" Immediately Blood Clot jumped on his horse and galloped away, changing as he did so into a buffalo. His wife cried and attempted to catch him, but in vain. From that time on, Blood Clot ran with the buffalo.

KUTENAI

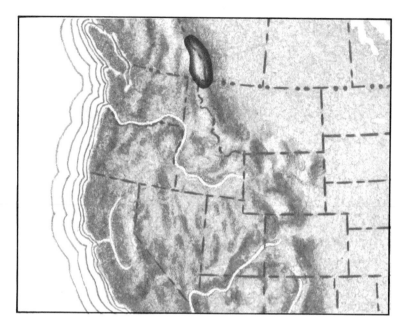

The Kutenai, who lived in a region of many lakes
and rivers, developed a sturdy and swift canoe that permitted them to travel
safely. They believed that many monsters and
other spirits lived in the lakes and forests and inhabited the
animals and objects around them.
One monster, Ya-woo-nik, was once
responsible for a great flood, and, in this story, the
Kutenai tell how the fish, birds, and animals got together to save the world
from watery destruction.

THE GREAT MONSTER AND THE GREAT FLOOD

In the days when the people all lived on the eastern side of Columbia Lake, they used to cross the water for huckleberries. One day, as they were returning, Duck and his wife were swallowed by a great monster, Ya-woo-nik, whose name means Deep Water Dweller. Duck's brother, Redheaded Woodpecker, having decided to summon all the fish in order to find out where this monster could be found, sent Dipper up every stream inviting all the fish to come, and he dispatched Snipe around the lake. Each messenger, whenever he stopped, called, "You fish are all invited to come! If you do not, we will dry this lake and you will all die!" So the fish gathered at the appointed place.

When they arrived, Woodpecker said to them, "I have lost my brother in this water. Ya-woo-nik has swallowed him. Now you fish must know where this Ya-woo-nik is. I want you to tell me where he is." Sucker responded, "I like to stay in the deep water on the bottom, and there I have seen him." Woodpecker immediately sent Long Legs, a kind of duck, to find Ya-woo-nik, but the water was too deep and he had to turn back.

At that moment, there appeared in the council a very tall person, so tall that had he stood upright, his head would have touched the sky. He was Nahlmokchi, and he was a person, not an animal. He had been traveling from the north to the south, stopping at each place to give it a name. Woodpecker requested him to drive the monster out of the depths, and the stranger waded into the lake. He kicked at Ya-woo-nik but missed him, and the monster fled into the river, up a small creek, and into the very source of the stream, under the mountain. After him crawled Nahlmokchi, who built a dam at the place where the monster had gone under the mountain. Woodpecker now placed his brother, Sapsucker, beside the dam and instructed him carefully, "When he comes out, say that Woodpecker is going to spear him. Then he will stop, and I will come around and kill him."

Woodpecker himself went to the other side of the mountain and kicked, and the monster started to come out. When he encountered the dam, Sapsucker, excited and confused, cried, "Sapsucker is going to spear you!" Ya-woo-nik broke through the dam, grunting, "Sapsucker! I am not afraid of your spear; I am going to swallow you!" Sapsucker turned and ran, but just at that moment, Woodpecker appeared and thrust at the monster with his bill. However, the monster had started to enter the stream below the dam so that he was only wounded in a foot. He hurried down the stream, leaving a trail of blood.

Woodpecker sent Beaver ahead to build a dam and stop him, and when Ya-woo-nik came to the obstruction, he could go no farther, and Wood-pecker came up and killed him. He ripped the monster's belly open, releasing Duck and his wife.

Water began to flow from Ya-woo-nik's wounds. His blood was water. It gradually spread over the earth until the people were forced to flee to the mountains. Still the water kept rising, and, at last, only one peak was left above the water. Chicken Hawk pulled out one of his spotted tail feathers and stuck it into the ground at the edge of the rising water. "Watch!" said he. "If the water goes above that last stripe, we shall die!" The water stopped at the last stripe then began to subside. After the water was gone, not all the people descended to the earth; the mountain birds began their life in the mountains at that time.

FLATHEAD

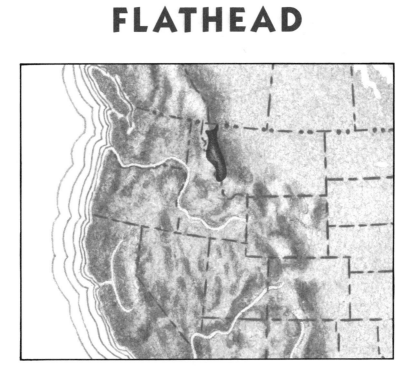

In this tale from the Flathead Indians of Montana, Coyote

uses his magic power to trick a cruel giant.

COYOTE KILLS A GIANT

One day, Coyote came upon a very sharp butte on top of which lay a Giant. Coyote had a little black squirrel for a dog and he called him One Ear. The Giant had a Grizzly Bear for his dog. Grizzly Bear killed all the people who passed through the valley and never missed one.

At the foot of the hill, Coyote saw a little camp of Mice. He said to them, "What will you take to dig a little hole for me from the bottom of this hill up to where the Giant is? I want to go up under the ground. It is the only way I can get up."

The Mice said, "Give us some blackberries and we will dig the hole." Then Coyote gave them some blackberries and they began to dig. They dug and dug until the hole reached from the foot of the hill to the top. It came right up to where the Giant lay.

Coyote went in about noon. He crawled through the little hole and, pretty soon, he came out right under the Giant's belly, where the hole ended.

The Giant was very much surprised. "Where did you come from?" he asked.

Coyote said, "Are you blind that you didn't see me come?"

"Which way did you come?" asked the Giant.

"I came right across the prairie," answered Coyote.

"I didn't see you," said the Giant. "I've been watching everywhere all day, and I didn't see anyone come."

Coyote said again, "Are you blind that you didn't see me? You must have been asleep. That is the

reason you didn't see me."

Just then, the dogs began to growl at each other. Coyote said to the Giant, "You had better stop your dog. My dog will kill him if you don't."

The Giant said, "You had better stop your dog. My dog will swallow him."

Then the two dogs began to fight. One Ear ran under Grizzly Bear and cut his belly open with his sharp-pointed ear. Grizzly Bear fell down dead.

Coyote said, "I told you to stop your dog. Now he is killed."

Then they sat down and began to talk. Coyote made a wish and whatever he wished always came true. He wished there were lots of horses and women and men down at the foot of the hill. Pretty soon he could see the people and horses moving down there. The Giant didn't see them yet.

Coyote said, "I thought you had good eyes."

The Giant said, "Of course I have good eyes. I can see everything."

Coyote answered, "You said you have good eyes. Can you see the Indians moving over there? You didn't see them yet?"

The Giant looked very carefully and he saw the Indians moving. He was ashamed that he didn't see them before.

"Now," said Coyote, "let us be partners. We will kill all these people."

"All right," answered the Giant.

"Now we will go after them," said Coyote. "We

will go down to the foot of the hill."

They started down the hill, and when they were halfway down, the Giant was very tired.

"Give me your knife," said Coyote. "I will carry it for you. It is too heavy for you, and you are already very tired." So the Giant gave Coyote his knife. Then they started on.

When they got to the bottom of the hill, the Giant said, "I am not going any farther than this. I am played out."

Coyote said, "Give me your bow and arrows. I will carry them for you." The Giant gave his bow and arrows to Coyote. Then he had nothing at all to fight with.

As soon as Coyote got the bow and arrows, he began to jump and yell. "Now we'll start war right here," he said.

"Let me go free, Coyote," begged the Giant. "I won't kill anymore people. I'll be good, good friends with everybody, if you let me go."

"No," said Coyote. "I am going to kill you now. Today is your last day."

Then he began to shoot his arrows, and soon the Giant fell down dead. From that day on, the valley of the Giant was safe for all.

PEND D'OREILLE

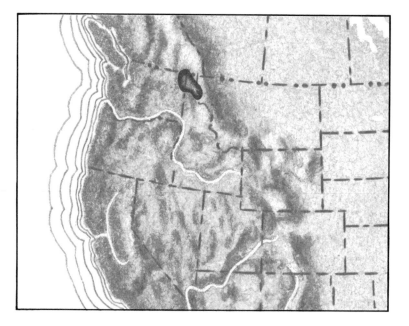

This story explains how Flying Squirrel got his
"wings," why Whitefish has a small, puckered mouth, and why Sucker
has so many bones.
The tribe that told this tale was known by many different names,
each of which tells something about the people
of the tribe.

THE WREN

The Earth people wanted to make war on the Sky people. Grizzly Bear was their chief, and he called all the warriors together. They were told to shoot in turn at the sky. All did as directed, but their arrows fell short.

Only Wren had not shot his arrow. Coyote said, "He need not shoot. He is too small, and his bow and arrows are too weak." However, Grizzly Bear declared that Wren must have his turn. Wren shot his arrow, and it hit the moon sky and stuck fast.

The others also shot their arrows, each of which stuck in the notch of the preceding one, until the arrows made a chain reaching from the ground to the sky. Then all the people climbed up, Grizzly Bear going last. He was very heavy, and when he was up more than halfway, the chain broke because of his weight. He sprang up and caught the part of the chain above him; this caused the arrows to pull out of the top where the leading warriors had made a hole to enter the sky. The whole chain fell down and left the people without means of descending.

The Earth people attacked the Sky people, the Stars, and defeated them in the first battle, but soon so many Stars gathered that they far outnumbered the Earth people and in the next battle routed them, killing a great many.

The defeated Earth people ran for the ladder, many being overtaken and killed on the way. When they found the ladder gone, each prepared himself the best way he could so as not to fall too heavily and one after another jumped down.

Flying Squirrel was wearing a small robe that he spread out like wings when he jumped. He came down without hurting himself; therefore, he has something like wings now.

Whitefish looked down the hole before jumping. When he saw how high up he was, he puckered up his mouth and drew back; therefore, he has a small puckered mouth to the present day.

Sucker jumped down without first preparing himself and his bones were broken; therefore, the Sucker's bones are found in all parts of his flesh now.

CALIFORNIA CULTURE AREA

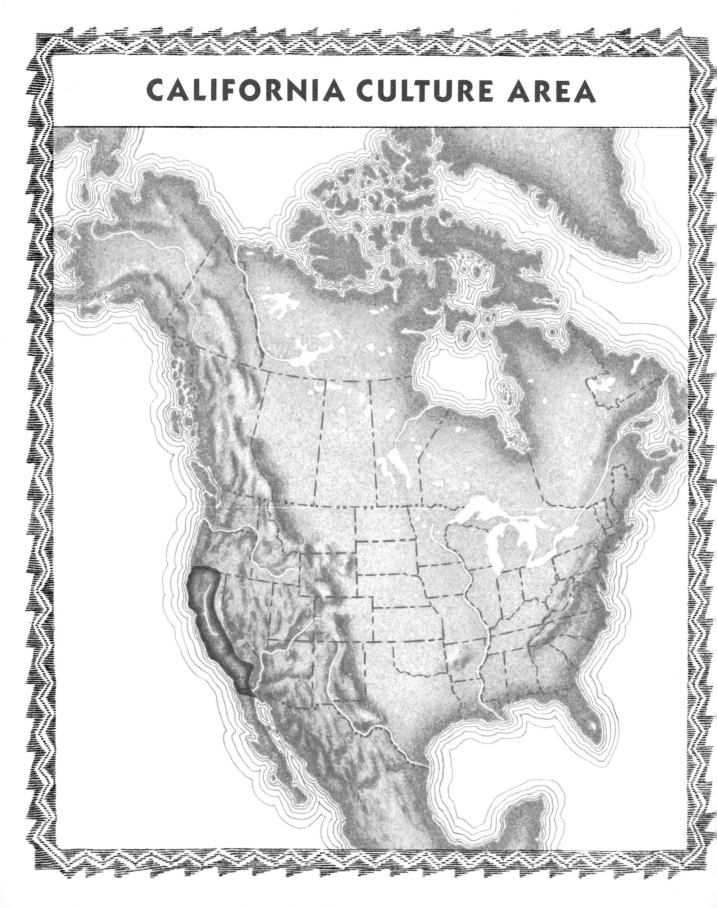

The California culture area included numerous tribes who lived in what is now the state of California, principally along the narrow coastal plain, along the lower parts of rivers, and in the warm interior valleys. Acorns were the staple food in the diet of many of these peoples. Agriculture did not develop. On the coast, fishing was a major occupation, while inland, hunting and gathering sustained life. These people seldom engaged in warfare and because of an abundance of food they had the time to develop a complex social and ceremonial life. Houses were usually dome-shaped, made of a framework of poles which were covered with earth, brush, bark, palm fronds, rush mats, or wooden slabs, depending on the materials available in particular areas. Large ceremonial round houses held major winter ceremonies where dancers impersonated different supernatural beings and acquired their power.

WINTU

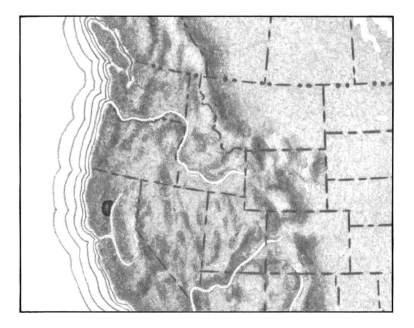

The Wintu believed that there were spirits, called
"kakeni," everywhere. Each kakeni lived in a particular rock, mountain, cave,
lake, or waterfall. All the birds and animals had
such a spirit counterpart, which could give supernatural powers
to ordinary mortals.
After the creation of the world and
everything in it, there was still darkness
everywhere, so the Wintu chose Blue Jay to bring light
to the world.

THE FIRST DAWN

Once the country was pitch-dark. The people had a meeting to find a fast runner. Finally they chose Blue Jay, who went eastward. He came to an earth lodge in a village where many people lived. All the people had gone off for a celebration a little distance away, and the only one left behind was a little boy.

Blue Jay went into the lodge and talked to the boy. He asked, "Where are all the people?" The boy answered, "They have gone away."

In the earth lodge were storage baskets set against the wall. Blue Jay pointed to the first basket and asked, "What is in that basket?" The boy said, "Early evening." Then Blue Jay pointed to the next basket and asked, "What is in that basket?" The boy an-swered, "Just dark." Blue Jay kept this up a long time. At last, he pointed to a basket and asked, "What is in that basket?" The boy said, "Dawn." Then Blue Jay seized the basket and ran away with it.

The boy shouted, "They have stolen our Dawn!" The people were dancing and paid no attention to the boy. At last someone said, "The boy is shouting that someone has stolen our Dawn," so they all ran over to the earth lodge and began following Blue Jay.

They followed him toward the west. He kept going west. Near Big Valley, they were catching up with him; they had almost caught him when he opened the basket and light flew out.

MAIDU

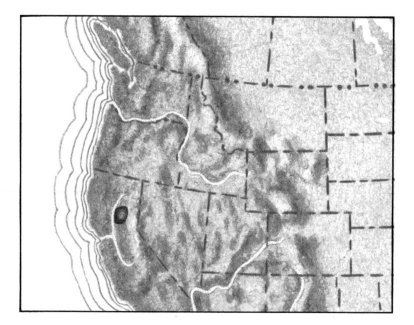

In this Maidu story, Earth Namer creates
the first people with Turtle's help.

EARTH NAMER AND THE CREATION

In the beginning, there was no sun, no moon, no stars. All was dark, and everywhere there was only water. A raft came floating on the water from the north, and in it were Turtle and Father-of-the-Secret-Society. The stream flowed very rapidly. Then from the sky a rope of feathers was lowered, and down it came Earth Namer. When he reached the end of the rope, he tied it to the raft. His face was covered and was never seen, but his body shone like the sun. He sat down on the raft and for a long time said nothing.

At last Turtle said, "Where do you come from?"

"I come from above," Earth Namer answered.

"Brother," Turtle asked, "can you make some good dry land for me so that I may sometimes come up out of the water?"

"If you want to have some dry land, I will need some earth to make it," said Earth Namer.

Turtle replied, "If you tie a rope around my left arm, I'll dive for some."

Earth Namer reached around, took the end of a rope from somewhere, and tied it to Turtle. When Earth Namer had come to the raft, there was no rope there; he just reached out and found one. "If the rope is not long enough," Turtle continued, "I'll jerk it once, and you must haul me up; if it is long enough, I'll give two jerks, and then you must pull me up quickly as I shall have all the earth I can carry."

Turtle was gone a long time! In fact, Turtle was gone six years, and when he came up, he was covered with green slime because he had been down so long. When he reached the surface of the water, the only earth he had was a little bit under his nails; the rest had all washed away. Earth Namer took a stone knife with his right hand from under his left armpit and carefully scraped the earth out from under the Turtle's nails. He put the earth, which was only the size of a small pebble, into the palm of his hand and rolled it about until it was round and then laid it on the stern of the raft.

By and by, he went to look at it, but it had not grown at all, but the third time that he went to look at it, it had grown so that it could be spanned by his arms. The fourth time he looked, it was as big as the world, the raft was aground, and all around were mountains as far as he could see. The raft came ashore at Todoiko, and the place can be seen today.

When the raft came to land, Turtle said, "I can't stay in the dark all the time. Can't you make some light so that I can see?"

"Let us get out of the raft," Earth Namer replied, "and then we will see what we can do."

So all three got out. Then Earth Namer said, "Look that way, to the east! I am going to tell my sister, the sun, to come up." It began to grow light, and day began to break; then Father-of-the-Secret-Society in his excitement began to shout loudly, and finally the sun came up.

"Which way is the sun going to travel?" Turtle asked.

Earth Namer answered, "I'll tell her to go this way," as he pointed to the west, "and go down there."

Later, after the sun went down, Father-of-the-Secret-Society began to shout again, and it grew very dark.

"I'll tell my brother to come up," Earth Namer said, and the moon rose.

Then Earth Namer asked Turtle and Father-of-the-Secret-Society, "How do you like it?"

"It is very good," they answered.

Then Turtle asked, "Is that all you are going to do for us?"

"No, I am going to do more." Then Earth Namer called the stars, each by its name, and they all came out.

When this was done, Turtle asked, "Now what shall we do?"

"Wait, and I'll show you," Earth Namer replied.

Then he made a tree grow and Earth Namer, Turtle, and Father-of-the-Secret-Society sat in its shade. The tree was very large and had twelve different kinds of acorns growing on it.

After they had sat for two days under the tree, they all went off to see the world that Earth Namer had made. They started at sunrise and were back by sunset. Earth Namer traveled so fast that all they could see was a ball of fire flashing about under the ground and the water.

While they were gone, Coyote and his dog Rattlesnake came up out of the ground. It is said that Coyote could see Earth Namer's face. When Earth Namer and the others came back, they found Coyote at Todoiko. All five of them then built huts for

themselves, and lived there, but no one could go inside of Earth Namer's house.

Soon after the travelers came back, Earth Namer called the birds from the air and made the rest of the trees and then the animals. He took some mud and of this made first a deer; after that he made all the other animals. Sometimes Turtle would complain, saying, "That does not look good; can't you make it some other way?"

Sometime after the animals were all formed, Earth Namer and Coyote were alone and Earth Namer said, "I am going to make people."

In the middle of the afternoon, he began by taking dark red earth, mixing it with water, and making two figures—one a man and one a woman. He laid the man on his right side and the woman on his left inside his house. Then he lay down himself, flat on his back, with his arms stretched out. He lay this way and sweated all afternoon and night. Early in the morning, the woman began to tickle him in the side. He kept very still, and he did not laugh.

The two people were very handsome, but it is said that Earth Namer did not finish the hands of the people as he did not know how it would be best to do it. Coyote saw the people and suggested that they ought to have hands like his.

"No," Earth Namer said, "their hands shall be like mine," and then he finished them.

When Coyote asked why their hands were to be like that, Earth Namer answered, "So that if they are chased by bears, they can climb trees."

This first man was called Kuksu and this first woman was named Morning-Star Woman. By and by, there came to be many, many more people on earth.

KAROK

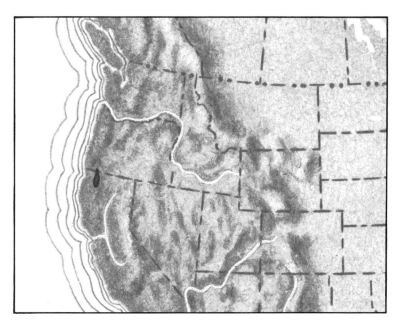

Kareya, "The Old Man Above," was the supreme

being of the Karok. Sitting on his sacred stool, he first created the world then

created fishes, animals, and, finally, man.

Somehow, in the creation process, Kareya prevented the Karok

from getting their main food, the salmon, by building

a dam.

Coyote solved the problem by stealing the key and opening the dam.

However, there was still a problem for the Karok:

There was no fire with which to cook the

fish. This next Karok tale continues the story.

THE ORIGIN OF FIRE

Far away, toward the rising sun, somewhere in a land that no Karok had ever seen, Kareya had made fire and hidden it in a casket, which he gave to two old hags to keep lest some Karok should steal it. So now Coyote befriended the Karok and promised to bring them some fire.

He went out and got together a great company of animals, one of every kind, from the lion down to the frog. These he stationed in a line all along the road, from the home of the Karok to the far-distant land where the fire was, the weakest animal nearest home and the strongest near the fire.

Then he took an Indian with him and hid him under a hill and went to the cabin of the hags who kept the casket and rapped on the door. One of them came out and he said, "Good evening," and they replied, "Good evening." Then he said, "It's a pretty cold night; can you let me sit by your fire?" And they said, "Yes, come in." So he went in and stretched himself out before the fire, reached his snout out toward the blaze, sniffed the heat, and felt very snug and comfortable. Finally, he stretched his nose out along his forepaws and pretended to go to sleep, though he kept the corner of one eye open, watching the old hags. But they never slept, day or night, and he spent the whole night watching and thinking to no purpose.

Next morning, he went out and told the Indian whom he had hidden under the hill that the Indian must make an attack on the hags' cabin as if he were about to steal some fire while Coyote was in the cabin. He then went back and asked the hags to let him in again, which they did, as they did not think a coyote could steal any fire. He stood close to the casket of fire, and when the Indian made a rush on the cabin and the hags dashed out after him at one door, Coyote seized a brand in his teeth and ran out the other door.

He almost flew over the ground, but the hags saw the sparks flying and gave chase, gaining on him fast. By the time he was out of breath, he had reached the lion, who took the brand and ran with it to the next animal, and so on, each animal barely having time to give it to the next before the hags came up.

The next to the last in the line was Ground Squirrel. He took the brand and ran so fast with it that his tail caught fire; he curled it up over his back and the fire caused the black spot we see to this day on his shoulders.

Last of all was Frog, but he couldn't run at all. So he opened his mouth wide, Squirrel chucked the fire into it, and Frog swallowed it down with a gulp. Then he turned and gave a great jump, but the hags were so close in pursuit that one of them grabbed him by the tail (he was a tadpole then) and tweaked it off. That is why frogs have no tails to this day.

Frog swam underwater a long distance, as long as he could hold his breath, then came up and spit out the fire into some driftwood. There it has remained safe since, so that whenever an Indian rubs two pieces of wood together, the fire comes forth.

MODOC

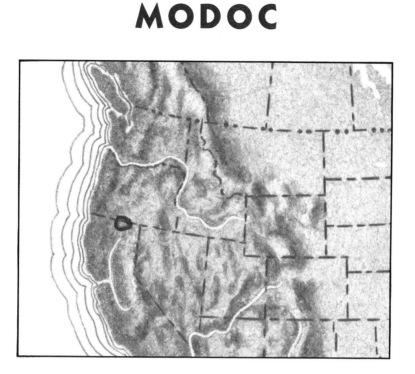

The Modoc still live in their native land at the foot

of the Cascade Mountains in California. Traditionally, the Modoc dug roots

from the earth, hunted game in the valleys, and

fished in the waters of the streams.

You can see in "The Great Spirit and the Grizzlies"

how very important their native setting

was to the Modoc.

THE GREAT SPIRIT AND
THE GRIZZLIES

The first thing the Great Spirit made was Mount Shasta. He pushed down snow and ice from the skies through a hole that he made in the blue heavens by turning a stone around and around until he made this great mountain. Then he stepped out of the clouds onto the mountaintop, descended, and planted the trees all around by putting his finger on the ground.

The sun melted the snow and the water ran down and nurtured the trees and made the rivers. After that, he made the fish for the rivers out of the small end of his staff. He made the birds by blowing some leaves that he took up from the ground among the trees. Next, he made the beasts out of the remainder of his stick, but he made the grizzly bear out of the big end, which made the grizzly bear master over all the other beasts.

The Great Spirit made the grizzly so strong that he feared the grizzly and would have to go up to the top of the mountain, out of sight of the forest, to sleep at night. The grizzly, who was much stronger and much more cunning at that time than now, might have attacked him in his sleep.

Afterward, the Great Spirit wished to remain on earth and make the sea and some more land, so he converted Mount Shasta into a great wigwam. He built a fire in the middle of it and made it a pleasant home. His family came down, and they all lived in the mountain.

One late and severe springtime, there was a great storm around the summit of Mount Shasta, and the Great Spirit sent his youngest and fairest daughter up to the hole in the top. He told her to speak to the storm that came up from the sea and tell it to be more gentle or it would blow the mountain over. He instructed her to do this quickly and not to put her head out because the wind would catch her hair and blow her away. He told her, "Just thrust out your arm and make a sign and then speak to the storm outside."

The child went quickly to the top and did as she was told. Just as she was about to return, she stopped, turned, and put her head out to look at the furious storm, which she had never before seen. The storm caught in her long, red hair and blew her out and away, down and down the mountainside. She could not fix her feet in the hard, smooth ice and snow, so she slid on and on, down to the dark belt of fir trees below the snow rim.

The grizzlies possessed all the wood and all the land, even down to the sea at that time, and were very numerous and very powerful. They were not exactly beasts then, although they were covered with hair, lived in caves, and had sharp claws; but

48

they walked on two legs, talked, and used clubs to fight with instead of their teeth and claws, as they do now.

At that time, there was a family of grizzlies living near the snow line. The father was out looking for food when, as he returned with his club on his shoulder and a young elk in his left hand, he saw the little child hiding under a fir bush, her long hair trailing in the snow and shivering with fright and cold. Not knowing what to make of her, he took her to the mother grizzly, who was very learned in all things, and asked her what this fair and frail thing was that he had found under a fir bush.

The mother grizzly told him to leave the child with her, and she decided to bring her up with her own children. The mother grizzly reared her, and the father grizzly went out everyday to get food for his family until they were all grown up and able to take care of themselves.

One day, the mother grizzly said to the father grizzly, "Our oldest son is quite grown up and must have a wife. Now, who shall it be but the little creature you found in the snow under the fir bush." So the grizzly father said that she was very wise, took up his club on his shoulder, and went out and killed some game for the marriage feast.

They married and were very happy and many children were born to them. But, being part of the Great Spirit and part of the grizzly bear, these children did not exactly resemble either of their parents but took somewhat of the nature and likeness of both. Thus was a new race created, for these children were the first Indians.

After many years, the mother grizzly felt that she soon must die. Fearing that she had done wrong in detaining the child of the Great Spirit, she could not rest until she had seen him and had restored to him his long-lost treasure and had asked his forgiveness.

She gathered together all the grizzlies and sent her eldest grandson to the summit of Mount Shasta, in a cloud, to speak to the Great Spirit and tell him where he could find his long-lost daughter.

When the Great Spirit heard this, he was so glad that he ran down the mountainside so fast and so strong that the snow was melted off in places and his steps remain to this day. The grizzlies went out to meet him by the thousands. As he approached, they stood apart in two great lines, with their clubs under their arms, and opened a lane through which he passed to the lodge where his daughter sat with her children.

When he saw the children and learned how the grizzlies that he created had betrayed him into the creation of a new race, he was very angry and frowned on the mother grizzly until she died on the spot. At this, the grizzlies all set up a dreadful howl. The Great Spirit took his daughter on his shoulder, and, turning to all the grizzlies, told them to hold their tongues, get down on their hands and knees, and so remain until he returned. They did as they were told. He then drove all the children out into the world, went out and up the mountain, and never returned to the timber anymore.

So the grizzlies could not rise up anymore nor use their clubs. From that time on, they have had to go on all fours like the other animals, except when they have to fight for their lives. Then the Great Spirit allows them to stand up and fight with their fists like men.

NORTHWEST PACIFIC COAST CULTURE AREA

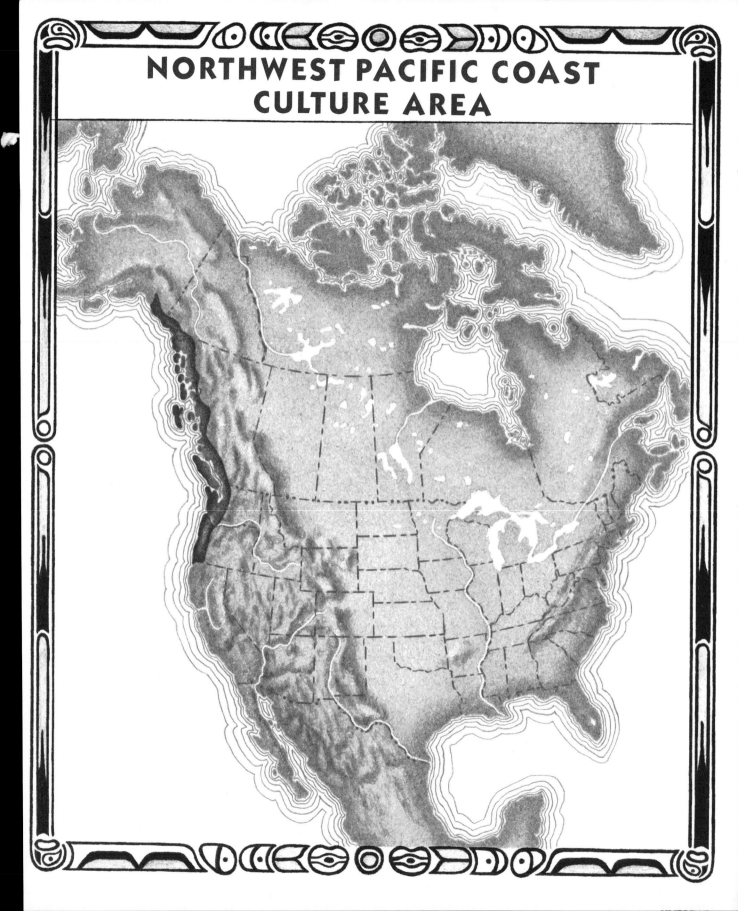

The Northwest Pacific Coast culture area extends along the coast from Prince William Sound in Alaska down into northern California. The people survived by fishing for salmon, halibut, and numerous other species that teemed in the coastal ocean waters. Marine mammals (whales, seals, sea lions, sea otters) were regularly hunted by some groups. The forests produced abundant supplies of berries, roots, and green vegetables as well as deer and elk—all heavily utilized. Agriculture never developed in this region. Northwest Coast longhouses were quite large and generally consisted of sturdy log frames covered with thick wooden planks. An abundant food supply allowed for the development of an elaborate social and ceremonial organization based on the accumulation of wealth, power, and status, and culminating in a major ceremony known as the potlatch. Here, in order to honor a particular person or event, a chief gave a huge feast followed by an elaborate ceremony in which he displayed his wealth in the form of objects, songs, and dances. He then gave away vast quantities of goods to specially invited guests, as well as to the crowd as a whole for witnessing the event.

TLINGIT

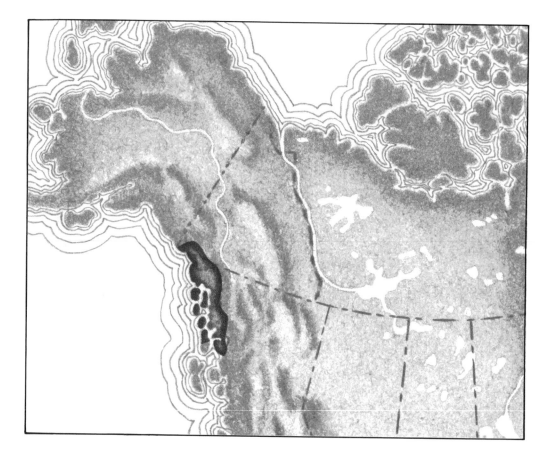

Many of the Tlingit stories explain things about nature. The tale about the "man in the moon" is the same as the Tlingit "girl with the water bucket." A young girl, on her way to collect water from a stream, unknowingly spoke harshly about the moon. As a punishment, she immediately went up to the moon, and the Tlingit say you can see her there now, holding her water bucket.

This next story from the Tlingit explains another natural occurrence; it tells why tree bark usually appears broken.

BEAVER AND PORCUPINE

The beaver and the porcupine were great friends and went about everywhere together. The porcupine often visited the beaver's house, but the beaver did not like to have him come because he left quills there.

One time, when the porcupine said that he wanted to go out to the beaver's house, the beaver said, "All right, I will take you out on my back." He started, but instead of going to his house, the beaver took him to a stump in the middle of the lake. Then he said to him, "This is my house," left him there, and went ashore.

While the porcupine was on this stump, he began singing a song, "Let it become frozen. Let it become frozen so that I can cross to the shore." So the surface of the lake froze, and he walked home.

Sometime after this, when the two friends were again playing together, the porcupine said, "You come now. It is my turn to carry you on my back." Then the beaver got on the porcupine's back, and the porcupine took the beaver to the top of a very high tree, after which the porcupine came down and left the beaver. For a long time, the beaver did not know how to get down, but finally he figured out a way to reach the ground. He faced the tree, spread his paws, and just slid down. As he descended, his sharp claws cut into the smooth bark of the tree.

They say that this is why tree bark has a broken appearance.

CHINOOK

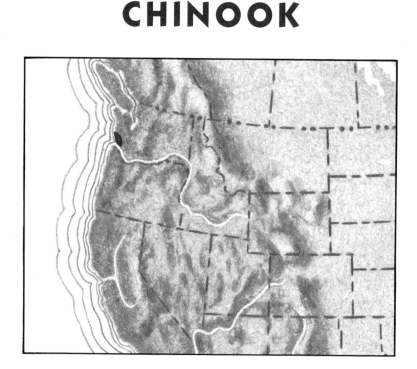

The medicine chant was a very important religious
occasion for the Chinook tribe. In this public ceremony, the special magic
powers given to a member of the tribe by a
spirit are revealed to all. This is done when the person sings the
song that was first learned when the magic power
was shared with him.

The next story tells about how the Raccoon came
to have slim, black paws. It is told through another story—that
of the medicine chant.

THE ANIMAL PEOPLE HOLD A
MEDICINE CHANT

All kinds of bird and animal people met at a village in the winter to sing their medicine songs. Grizzly Bear was the first. Everybody was afraid of him. He sang and danced, and each time he came near the fire, he slapped it and made coals, smoke, and wood fly into the air and shower down on the others, but no one dared say a word.

"If anybody interferes with what I am doing, I will eat his head, bones and all!" declared Grizzly Bear, and to show his bravery, he again slapped the fire. The others lowered their heads and said nothing, for they were all in fear of such a powerful creature.

A small lizard sat there. By and by, he cried, "I am going to stop him!" He walked forward quickly while Grizzly Bear was singing and said, "You are going too far, Grizzly Bear! We all know your name. You say that if anybody interferes, you will eat his head. You slap the fire and burn us. Your name is big enough, and you ought not to do this. I think you are not a good creature; you are a bad fellow!"

Grizzly Bear turned around and glowered at the little one; then he growled, "Who is this interfering?" He slapped the fire again and said, "I want to know who is doing this talking; I will eat him!"

"Here I am," said the one who had spoken; "look right at me! If you are foolish enough to eat me, I will make you drop everything there is in you!"

Grizzly Bear looked at the other closely and, recognizing him as Lizard, he said, "Oh, you are my relative, and I do not like to have trouble with you here. People all over the country would have the news that we have been fighting. They will say that Grizzly Bear and his brother were quarreling at the medicine singing." Grizzly Bear then sat down, for he feared Lizard.

Another came forward and sang, making a rattling, buzzing sound. This was Rattlesnake. "Let nobody interfere while I sing." He started to sing: "I do not know where I shall bite first; I do not know whom I shall bite first."

All the creatures remained quiet. About the middle of the song, a voice was heard: "Stop that 'Where I am going to bite; whom I am going to bite,' you flat-nosed thing! Other people here want to sing, and you must not take up all the time!" Rattlesnake began to rattle angrily so that for a time no other sound could be heard. The people were frightened and urged the one who had spoken, "Go out and show yourself; he may bite any of us!"

So Raccoon came out and said, "I am the one who spoke. If you bite me, I will burn out your eyes!" Rattlesnake turned and looked closely, then he said, "Why, we are relations, and I do not wish to have trouble in this gathering." So Rattlesnake withdrew.

Then Black Bear came out to sing, and he was

followed by the other animals and by all the plant people. At last, it was nearly spring when Crow started his song. The West Wind started to blow, the snow began to melt, and it was spring when Crow finished.

Lizard went home among the rocks, and one day he sat on the sunny side, making arrows. Grizzly Bear came along and looked, shading his eyes from the sun, and said, "There is the one who interfered with me at the singing." He went around and approached from the back. Lizard knew he was coming but paid no attention. He sat in a crevice. Something seized him by the head and pulled him back. He looked up and saw Grizzly Bear.

"Do you remember what you said to me at the singing?" asked Grizzly Bear.

"I do not remember saying anything to you," said Lizard.

"Now tell me what you said to me at that time," persisted Grizzly Bear. He growled fiercely and repeated, "Tell me!" and raised his paw to hit Lizard. Just then, Lizard slipped from his grasp, darted into a crack, and came up a moment later from another crevice, armed with bow and arrows and dressed for a fight.

Grizzly Bear leaped toward him again, and slapped at him, but Lizard darted into a crack and shot Grizzly Bear with one of his arrows. In this manner, the fight continued, Grizzly Bear leaping about and Lizard shooting little arrows into his body. After a while, Grizzly Bear fell dead, and Lizard cut off his claws. Down the breast of Grizzly ran a strip of white fur, which Lizard also cut off to use in his medicine making.

One day, Raccoon was down in the creek feeling under the stones for little suckers and crawfish. Rattlesnake saw him and recognized in him the one who had interrupted his singing. He determined to have revenge. He went to the edge of the water and waited, unseen, and after a while, Raccoon came that way, thrust his paw into the crack where Rattlesnake was waiting, and got bitten.

He did not notice this. He put his paw in again and was bitten five times. His paw began to swell and, thinking he must have gotten into some thorns, he built a fire and held his paw in it until the swelling was reduced. Then, happening to look around, he saw Rattlesnake, and aware now of the cause of his wounds, he picked him up and burned his eyes.

The fire is what made Raccoon's paws so black and slim.

NOOTKA

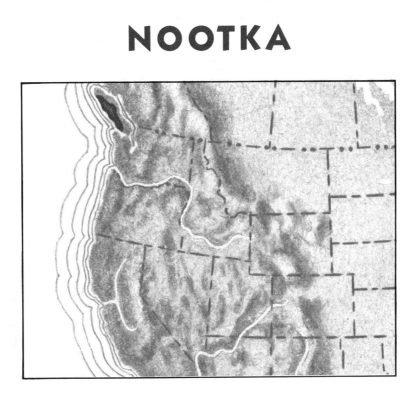

A fairly common belief among the Indians in
different parts of the continent was that thunder and lightning were caused
by Thunderbirds. These were thought of as
birds of enormous size who flapped their wings to produce
thunder and opened and closed their eyes to create lightning.
Some Nootka believed that at one time there had been
four Thunderbirds, all brothers.
This story explains how only one of the four
thunderbird brothers, Tototsh, survived after a series of encounters with
Woodpecker, Kingfisher, and Kwatyat, the trickster.

REDHEADED WOODPECKER AND THE THUNDERBIRDS

The Thunderbirds decided to play the hoop game and went to Maakoa, where Woodpecker lived. Woodpecker invited those who were to play the hoop game to a feast. Awipikwas, Woodpecker's wife, took out her salmonberry dish, said the magic words, "Kawi, kawi, kawi, kawi, kawi," and the berry dish filled up. Tototsh, who was the oldest of the Thunderbirds, was watching Awipikwas give out the salmonberries to the hoop players, and, as she passed him while he was eating his salmonberries, he fell in love with her.

After they had eaten, the players got ready to start the hoop game, and all four gathered together. Black Bear, who was the Thunderbirds' hoop thrower, was the first to play. Crane, the Thunderbirds' best marksman in spearing, stood by. Woodpecker had his players ready; he had Kingfisher for spearing and Kwatyat for hoop throwing. The players took their places and got ready for the game.

The Thunder people were the first to throw the hoop; it was Black Bear, the strong one, who tossed first. At the same time that he threw the hoop, the Thunderbirds made hail and lightning so that the hoop was lost to sight. The only one who could see it was Kingfisher, the sharp-eyed one. He threw his spear, and the point came off and stuck in the hoop.

Then it was the turn of the Woodpecker's hoop thrower; Kwatyat, the one of many tricks, got ready to throw the hoop. Blowing into his hoop to give it power, he said, "Get small; get small!" and the hoop became small at once. He threw the hoop, and Crane, the Thunderbird's marksman, missed his aim.

Black Bear in his turn set the hoop going again, and Kwatyat again blew magic into it. "Grow big; grow big," said he, and the hoop got big. Again Kingfisher stuck the hoop with his spear. Four times they rolled the hoop on each side, and Kingfisher's spear never missed. The Thunder people were beaten.

Because of this defeat, Tototsh, the Thunderbird who thundered now and then, became angry. He made a great hail and thunder storm and took Awipikwas, Woodpecker's wife, along with him as he flew back to his home.

It became the time for the run of the salmon. Woodpecker changed himself into a nice little young spring salmon and swam into Tototsh's trap. The Thunderbird, along with his new wife, went out to see his trap. When he got there, he discovered the young salmon (who was really Woodpecker) in the trap. He threw the fish into the canoe and gave it to his wife. The little young spring salmon spoke. "It is I, your husband, Woodpecker. Eat me all alone, won't you? And then you shall throw my leftover bones into the water," said he.

After Thunderbird and his wife arrived at their home, Awipikwas roasted the little spring salmon on a spit. She ate it all by herself and, when she finished eating, she threw the bones into the water just as she had been told to do. She kept walking farther and farther into the water until Woodpecker was able to get her and finally take her home.

"I shall have my revenge," said Woodpecker, "on Thunderbird, the one who deprived me of my wife." He spoke to Kwatyat: "Go to the whale and borrow his diver skin." After Kwatyat returned with the skin, Woodpecker and Kwatyat went into the diver and went out to sea.

It was early morning when they arrived at the place where the Thunderbirds lived. The whale came up out of the water. The Thunder people who were sitting on the shore looked out and saw the great whale and one said, "Go, some of you, and wake up Nonopitshmik, the Thunderbird who catches the whales who come out once in a while." Nonopitshmik tried to seize the whale in his claws, but he was unable to lift him.

Nopitashil, the great sea hunter Thunderbird, came near to help his older brother, but, together, they could not lift the whale. Kwatyat, the one who knew many tricks, had said while inside the canoe-whale, "Get heavy; get heavy," and the whale had gotten so heavy that the two Thunderbird brothers could not lift him up. Then, between their talons, Woodpecker cut them into slits.

Now Lolotshap, the next to youngest Thunderbird brother, came to help, but like the other two, he could not do much with his claws. Finally, Tototsh, the oldest, went to help his younger brothers, but just then, one of them spoke. "Do not come to help! You alone shall remain alive. There is something wrong with us; we are as though our limbs are dying."

"Get heavy; get heavy! Get big; get big!" said Kwatyat, and the whale grew heavier and heavier. Then the three brothers together sank into the water and died. The oldest, Tototsh, the Thunderbird who thundered now and then was the only one to remain alive.

This is how Woodpecker had his revenge on those who had wronged him in taking away his wife. Woodpecker went home with Kwatyat and returned the whale diver skin. This is how he had his revenge, and it is for this reason that only one Thunderbird is left alive: He who thunders now and then.

HAIDA

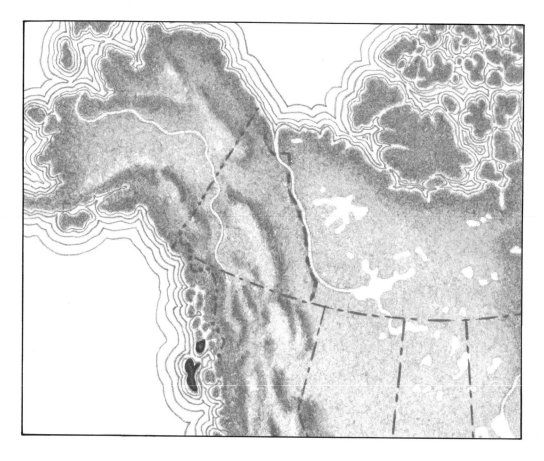

The Haida believed in a supreme being named

Nekilstlass, who took the form of a raven. He was the creator and preserver

of everything and the common father of all.

All of mankind descended from his marriage to a cockle, which

is a bivalve sea creature with a heart-shaped shell.

This next story tells how this creator

gave light to the world.

RAVEN LIGHTS THE WORLD

Nekilstlass had no beginning; neither will he have an end. In the shape of Raven before this world existed, he brooded over the immense darkness until, after countless ages, by the constant flapping of his wings, he beat down the darkness into solid earth. After the earth became solid, the light on its surface was dim and misty, so Raven went traveling far and wide to find some way to light it up.

During his travels, he heard of a chief who lived far away who had the sun, moon, and stars in three separate boxes. Raven went to this chief and asked him to give him the boxes, which the chief refused to do. While Raven was there, he saw that the chief had a pretty daughter, so he went away and turned himself into a handsome boy and wandered back to the chief's house. When the chief saw him, he told him to come in and stay a while, which the boy did.

After a while, the boy and girl fell in love, and the girl begged her father to let the boy have one of the boxes, the one that held the stars. Then, a little while later, in the same manner, he got the second box, which held the moon. Afterwards he begged hard for the box that held the sun. This the chief at first refused to part with, but after repeated requests from the young people, he at last let it go.

As soon as Raven possessed all the boxes, he placed them on high, where they have been ever since, giving light to the world.

ESKIMO CULTURE AREA

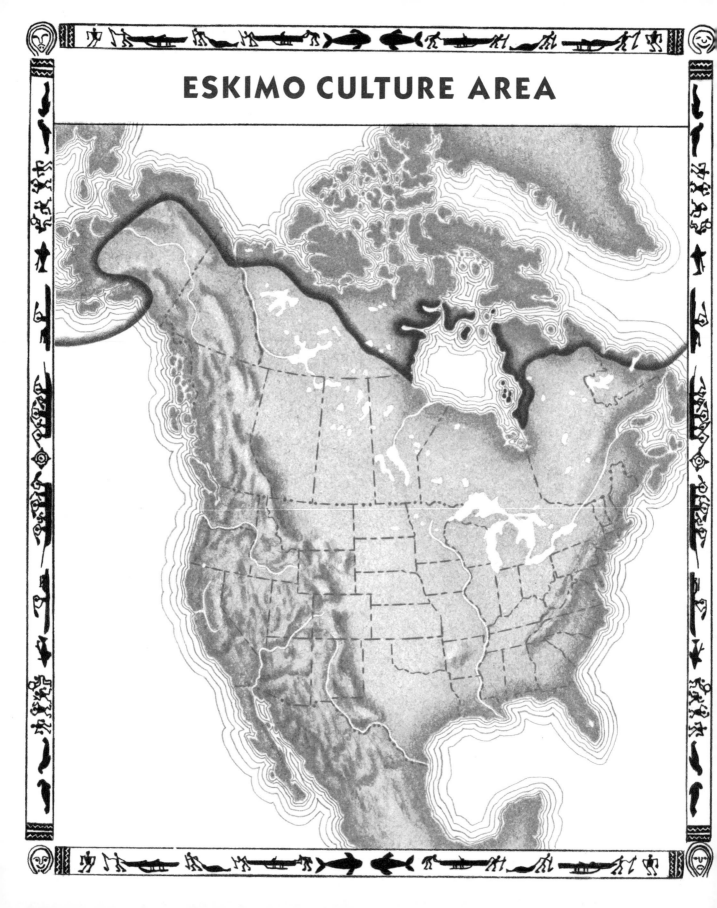

The Eskimo culture area includes the northernmost part of North America from the Aleutian Islands in the west, across Alaska, the Canadian Arctic, and western Greenland. In this most inhospitable climate, the Eskimos were primarily hunters—those along the coast hunted seal,  walrus, and whale. Those who lived inland sought caribou and other land game. Sometimes the groups migrated seasonally in order to take advantage of both hunting possibilities. In summer almost all groups lived in tents made of poles covered with skins. In the winter, Eskimos in the east built stone houses, while those in the west used driftwood and sod. The igloo (ice house) was found in northernmost Canada in the winter, but was seldom seen in Alaska. Shamans cured  illness and also produced good weather and lots of animals for the hunters.

NUNIVAK ESKIMO

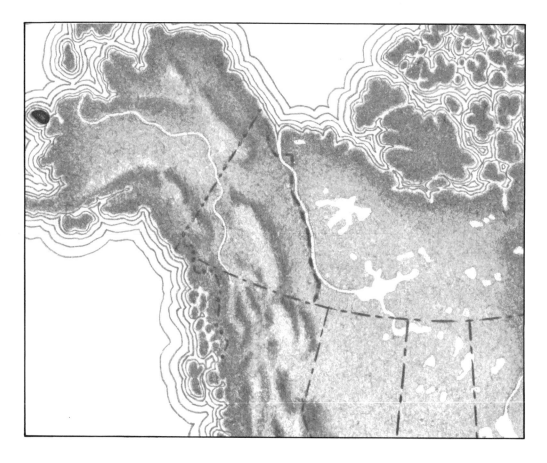

The Nunivak believed that spirits, in the
form of birds, animals, or objects, could enter a human body and give it
supernatural power. The recipient would then
become an important person in his village. He would take charge
of ceremonies, give advice, and distribute charms
and amulets, which were supposed to
contain supernatural powers. Those who received
the special power had to obey the spirits.

SPIDER COMES TO EARTH

There lived in the sky a spider who had as neighbors a sea gull and a hawk. Often, when alone in her house, Spider rolled aside her log headrest and watched the people on earth. Far below, there was a village in which lived a great hunter. The village was industrious, especially in the spring when the inhabitants were intent with preparations for the seal catch.

When all down below were making ready for the Bladder Feast, Spider spotted two of the most industrious people, the great hunter and his wife. The man she could see clearly, but the wife seemed to be enveloped in a haze or mist. Spider's heart was filled with desire. She muttered, "I wish I could go down there and marry that man. I shall be here alone until my time to die comes. That will be bad. I wish that man were my husband."

Again, looking down at the village, Spider saw the Bladder Feast being held. The man, the great hunter, was transparent to her. She could see through him, although there was one dark spot in his body, which was his stomach. Spider made up her mind. She told her neighbors, Sea Gull and Hawk, "I have been alone all my life. Now I am going down to earth. You must be ready to help me if I am attacked."

That night, while the people were singing the new songs in the men's house on earth, Spider swung down on her long thread. As she landed, the women came out of the men's house. Spider hid by the path and quickly killed the great hunter's wife as she passed Spider's place of concealment. Spider then followed the women to the women's house, where she cooked food. With the other women, she carried a bowl of food to the men's house and laid it at the feet of the great hunter. She lived with the hunter as his wife and nobody noticed that Spider was not his real wife.

One day, the hunter, now her husband, said, "You must be very careful in what you do. I know that you are not the wife I had before and that her relatives suspect you. She had five brothers and five uncles. The youngest brother is the child who often comes here. Those people wish to know where their relative has gone."

Soon Spider had a child by her husband, and then he warned her, "These people are trying to kill you. You have no chance to get away."

One night, while Spider was walking with her child, she saw something sparkle on the ice far ahead of her. The sparkle traveled toward her, and soon she saw that it was a whale, plowing through the snow as whales push aside water with their blunt snouts. Spider was frightened and thought of her neighbor, Sea Gull. As the whale approached near enough to strike, Sea Gull flew down and harpooned it with his long beak.

The next morning, when she awoke, her husband said, "How did you escape the uncles and the brothers of my former wife? You must be very careful now, for her father is searching for you. Perhaps I had better stay by you while you are in trouble."

"No," Spider answered, "you must stay in the men's house."

That night, Spider tied her child on her back and walked over the snow. Again she saw a sparkle on the snow, moving toward her. As it approached, she saw that it was a beast with a serrated back, cutting through the frozen ground as easily as if it were swimming through water. Spider thought, "Now I am in trouble and need help."

As the beast was about to strike her, she heard the thunder of wings and the wild screech of a hawk. Hawk swooped down and killed the strange beast with a thrust of his beak.

In the morning, her husband said, "How do you escape the ferocious animals sent to kill you? The relatives of my former wife are very angry because they all have the power to conjure up beasts and evil spirits. The next attempt will be the strongest because all will work together."

Spider was then so frightened that her teeth chattered. That night, when she opened the smoke hole, all the brothers and uncles of the former wife entered the house. They said to her, "You have killed all the beasts, the evil spirits, that we have sent against you. Now we ourselves are going to kill you!"

In her fright, Spider thought of Sea Gull and Hawk. As each one of the relatives came to grab her, Sea Gull and Hawk, poking their heads through the smoke hole, killed them with their beaks, sparing only the youngest brother. That one said, "I told my uncles and brothers not to try to kill you, but they did not listen to me."

The boy lived with them until he was grown and old enough to take a wife. Then her husband told Spider, "That youngest brother, to avenge his relatives, will try to kill you. You must be very careful."

Spider replied, "I am tired of being hunted and of people trying to kill me. Tonight I shall return to the sky. You must remain on earth because this is your home."

The husband felt very bad. He wanted to go with her because he did not want to be alone on earth. At night, Spider made preparations to leave, lashing the child securely on her back. After much pleading, Spider permitted her husband to go with her. She went up into the sky, dragging him after her. There they lived happily, often pulling aside the head log to watch the people on earth. Sea Gull and Hawk entered the body of the husband and became his supernatural powers.

BAFFIN ISLAND ESKIMO

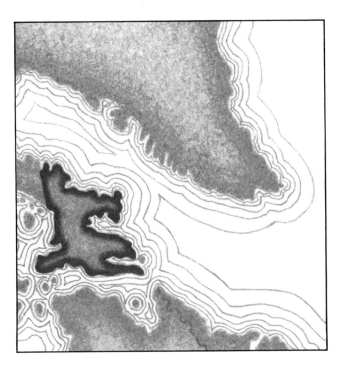

Many of the Baffin Island Eskimos believed that after death the souls
of those who had led a good life on earth went to a kind of paradise, which was
below ground, while those who had led a life of evil
went to an upper land of misery. In the good land below, there was a continuous
summer, plenty of fresh water, and unlimited game.
The souls of those who had been lazy, evil, or unfit for working went to the
upper world. There, as this next tale shows,
they were forever tormented by ravens.

THE OWL AND THE RAVEN

The owl and the raven were fast friends. One day, the raven made a new dress, dappled white and black, for the owl. The owl, in return, made a pair of boots of whalebone for the raven and then began to make a white dress. When she was about to try it on, the raven was hopping about and would not sit still. The owl got angry and said, "Now sit still or I shall pour out the lamp over you."

As the raven continued hopping about, the owl lost her temper and poured the contents of her lamp over the raven. Then the raven cried, "Qaq! Qaq!" and since that day he has been black all over.

SOUTHEAST GREENLAND ESKIMO

Storytellers would often help pass the time during

the long winter months of darkness. Families would gather together to listen

to the traditional tales, many of which went on for hours.

A skillful narrator could embellish his story so well that most of his

listeners would fall asleep before he finished telling it.

The best of the storytellers bragged that some of their tales were never heard to the end.

But some stories were quite short. In this next brief tale

about ravens, there is a commonly found character, one who has magic

powers that are used to create or alter natural phenomena.

WHEN THE RAVENS COULD SPEAK

Once, long ago, there was a time when the ravens could talk, but the strange thing about the ravens' speech was that their words had the opposite meaning. When they wanted to thank anyone, they used mean words of abuse and thus always said the reverse of what they meant.

But as they were thus so full of lies, there came one day an old man who by magic means took away their power of speech. Since that time, the ravens can do no more than shriek.

The ravens' nature has not changed, and to this day, they are an ill-tempered, lying, thieving lot.

KODIAK ESKIMO

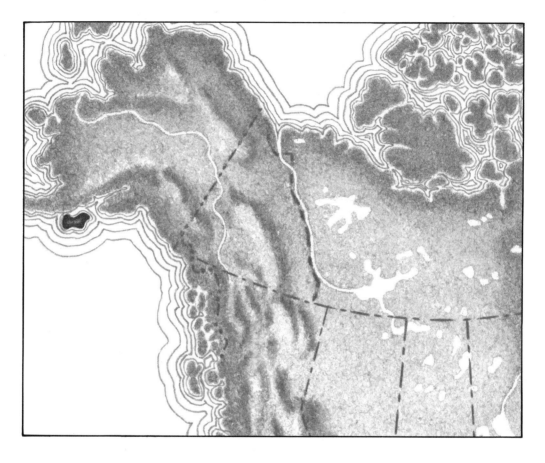

According to one of the first Europeans to visit the Kodiak Eskimos in the early 1800's, the inhabitants had many different stories about their origin. One told of a large canoe that fell from the sky with all the people in it. Another told of the Kodiak Eskimos being the descendants of a she-dog from the island who had mated with a he-goat from the mainland. Other stories described how the animals got their different traits. The next story, for instance, tells how the squirrel came to make many holes in which to store food.

HOW SQUIRRELS CAME TO MAKE MANY HOLES

The braggart Crow, always hungry, one day saw Squirrel picking berries. Crow's cunning thoughts told him to wait by Squirrel's hole. Soon Squirrel darted in great haste to his hole, for he knew that a fox had caught his scent. Squirrel stopped short when he saw Crow, knowing that the hungry bird would snatch him. He thought rapidly, then said, "O, Crow, with your beautiful glossy feathers, if you will sing and dance for me I shall give you the fat from my right side."

Crow, his vanity tickled, began to prance about, but always between Squirrel and the hole. Squirrel cried, "Dance harder, O, Crow, and shut your eyes! That is a fine dance!"

Crow obeyed because he liked to show off to anyone who would watch him. Squirrel applauded and said, "O, Crow, how well you dance! If you would only spread out your beautiful wings!"

The pleased Crow stretched and stiffened his wings until they rasped the ground. Squirrel then seized his opportunity and scuttled under the wings into his hole. The tricked and chagrined Crow, with anger in his heart at being so cozened, choked down his rage and called in honeyed tones to Squirrel, "Come out again, little partner. The sun is high and it is time to dance and play!"

Squirrel, in safety, merely laughed to himself. All summer, Crow lay in wait and Squirrel refused to come out. He grew very hungry but took the edge from his appetite by eating his nest. One morning, frost came, so Squirrel stuffed the entrance to his hole and went fast asleep. Crow, though ravenous, would not give up and decided to wait all winter, if necessary, through storm and calm.

Winter passed, and the trickling of melting snow awakened Squirrel. He knew that spring had come once more. Hunger seized him; he determined to go out. He tore down the stuffing that blocked his hole and peered out very cautiously. There he was reminded of his enemy. He saw the bones of Crow picked clean by the foxes. All summer, Squirrel thought of the hunger he was made to suffer through Crow and dared not go far from the safety of his retreat. The idea came to Squirrel to make many holes to run to in case of danger. Then he could increase his range and obtain more food. Today, all squirrels dig many holes to which they can scuttle whenever Crow, Fox, or other enemies approach.

SUB-ARCTIC CULTURE AREA

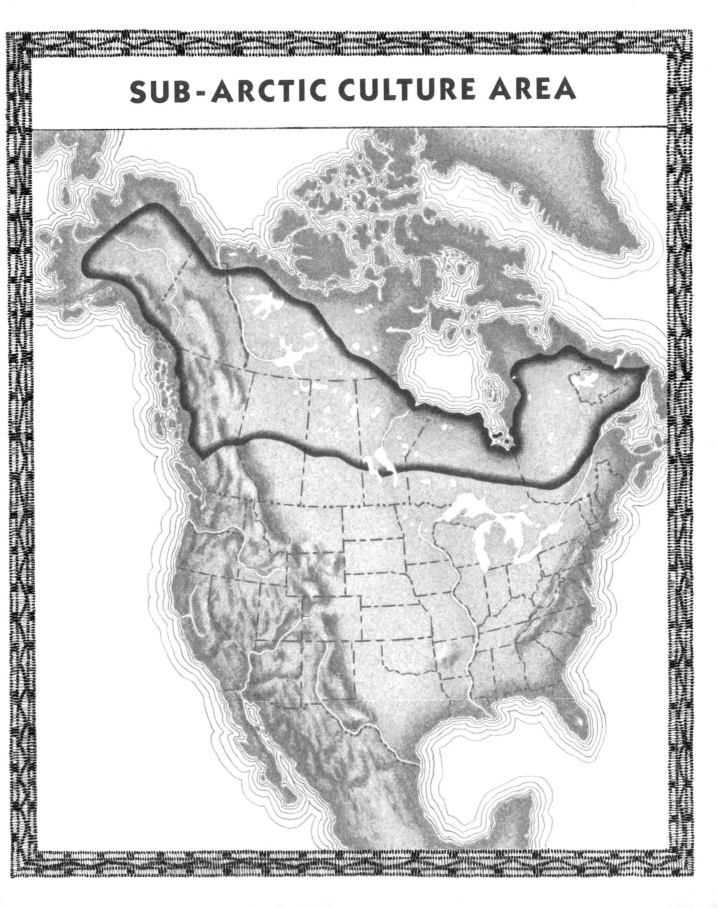

 The Sub-Arctic culture area lies just south of the Eskimo area, stretching from interior Alaska and the Canadian Rockies to Labrador and Newfoundland. These people survived by hunting moose, caribou, musk oxen, and elk, as well as other game animals.

They caught fish, killed a variety of birds and waterfowl for food, and foraged for roots and berries. In the western part of this area the people built plank houses similar to those of the Northwest Coast peoples. Some tribes lived in underground houses, while others made conical frameworks of poles covered with brush, bark, or skins. Tents were often  used in the summer. Powerful shamans healed diseases and could bring good or evil upon the people. Personal spirits, dreams, and visions were also important.

CARRIER

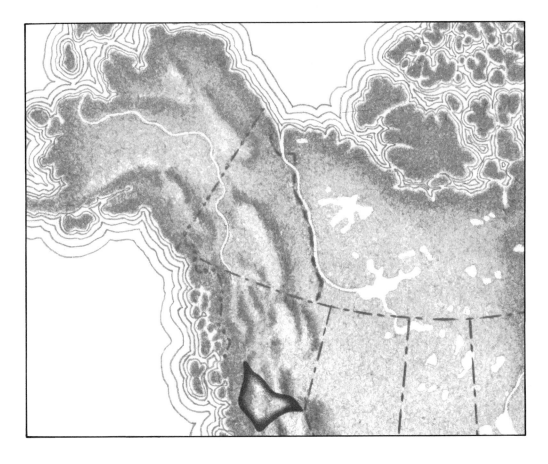

The Carriers lived along the Fraser River in British Columbia. Their name came from the tribal custom of burning their dead. If a married man died, his widow was required to remain on her husband's funeral pyre until the flames reached her. She then left the flaming body and, when the ashes cooled, collected them in a basket. She carried the basket for three years, and acted as a servant for her dead husband's family. Afterwards, a feast was held. The widow was released from servitude and permitted to remarry. The next story shows how Carrier people were seriously concerned with the mystery of death.

ORIGIN OF DEATH AND THE SEASONS

Frog and a small black insect had a discussion about men. Frog plucked a stalk of wild rhubarb and placed it on the bottom of a pool. When it floated to the surface, Frog said, "So may man rise again after he dies." The insect threw a stone into the water and said, "When man dies, may he remain dead, just as this stone remains at the bottom." The insect won.

On another occasion, Frog and Dog conversed together. Frog had three fingers; Dog had five.

Frog, speaking first, held out his three fingers and said, "Let winter last three months only, and let the rest of the year be summer." But Dog held out his five fingers and said, "Let summer last five months and winter last five."

Frog, angry at losing again, struck Dog's hand between the thumb and first finger so that now a dog's thumb is lower down on its hand than the other fingers.

Winter, too, lasts for five months.

CHIPEWYAN

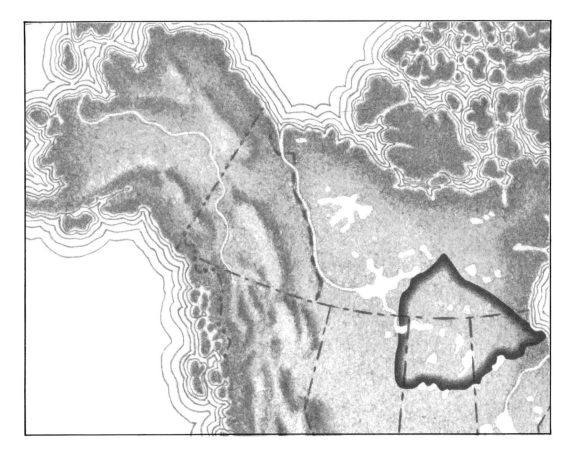

The Chipewyan were a very imaginative and poetic people in their interpretation of the natural world around them. For example, they would say, "Trees grow side by side so that they will never be lonely" and "A river drops through rapids or becomes a waterfall so that it will not get bored traveling over the same, quiet riverbed." Chipewyan stories were often about cranky bears, smart squirrels, wise beavers, and cunning crows. In "White Bear and Black Bear," the Chipewyan explain why the two kinds of bear no longer live together.

WHITE BEAR AND BLACK BEAR

Once upon a time, there was a White Bear and his nephew, Black Bear, who was staying with him, along with several other animals, including Fox. As Fox was always up to mischief, White Bear took away his right shoulder, and Fox became very ill. White Bear took Fox's shoulder and, along with a bunch of claws that he always carried, tied it up.

Fox, being very sick and not able to get along very well without his shoulder, sent for Crow, who was full of cunning, to devise some means of getting his shoulder back. After a long talk, Crow went to visit White Bear, who was very old and infirm and troubled with rheumatism. He was sitting at the fire, warming his back, when Crow came in. The bunch of claws and Fox's shoulder were hanging from the roof above his head.

Crow began to talk to him. Occasionally, he would touch the bunch of claws and White Bear would wake up with a start, at which Crow would explain that he was only touching the claws to see what they were made of. At last, White Bear took no notice of the noise and soon was half asleep. Crow, seeing his chance, caught hold of Fox's shoulder, pulled it down, and ran out of the camp.

White Bear then woke up and asked his nephew, Black Bear, what was the matter, and Black Bear, who stuttered, explained that Crow had run away with Fox's shoulder. He took so long in telling it that White Bear got angry and told Black Bear to get out and find a home for himself. Ever since, the white and black bears have lived apart.

Next, White Bear, to show his rage, took down the sun and put it with the claws. Now, as everything was in darkness, the other animals could not hunt and were starving, so they asked Crow to get them out of their trouble.

In the meantime, White Bear's daughter went for water and, as she was having a drink, she swallowed something black that was floating in the water. Some days afterward, a child was born to her. The infant grew so fast that soon he could walk about, and when he saw this bright thing hanging among the bunch of claws, he began to cry for it.

After much persuasion, White Bear gave it to him to play with in the camp. After a while, he wished to play outside with it, but White Bear would not at first allow it. As the child kept continually crying to be allowed to do so, he at last consented. He told him not to go far from the camp and, if he saw anybody coming, to run into the tepee at once. This the child promised to do, but as soon as he got out, he threw the sun up into the sky and flew away, for he was Crow in disguise.

When White Bear saw that he was cheated again by Crow, he was furious, and since then, white bears have always been wicked.

KASKA

The Kaska were part of a group of Indians who
lived in northern British Columbia and the Yukon. Wolverines were fairly
common in this part of North America, and
this Kaska tale explains how this animal got its reputation
as a thief.

WOLVERINE THE THIEF

Wolverine and Wolf were brothers-in-law and lived together. Wolf had no wife while Wolverine had a large family. They hunted together, Wolf crossing the high mountains, and Wolverine following the timberline below him. Game was very scarce. By and by, the deep snow prevented their hunting on the high grounds, and they had to hunt lower down in the woods, where game was still abundant.

One day, they came upon a cache of dried meat made by some people in a steep place near a waterfall and beyond their reach. Wolverine was very anxious to get at the cache and thought that by jumping against it, he might knock it down. Wolf could not attempt it and declared that if Wolverine jumped, he would not reach the cache and would simply fall down on the steep, smooth ice below and perhaps kill himself. Wolf declared that he was going home, and, just as he was leaving, Wolverine made the jump.

He fell short of the cache, landed on the steep ice, and fell to the bottom, breaking his arms and legs. Wolf lifted him up, but he could not get him out of there nor set his broken limbs. Soon afterward, some people came along to get meat from the cache and found Wolverine lying there with his arms and legs broken. They knew that he had been trying to steal, so they clubbed and killed him.

As he was dying, he said to the people, "No matter if you kill me, I shall steal from your caches just the same. There are many of us."

This is why the wolverine is such a thief and breaks into people's caches and steals their meat.

SLAVEY

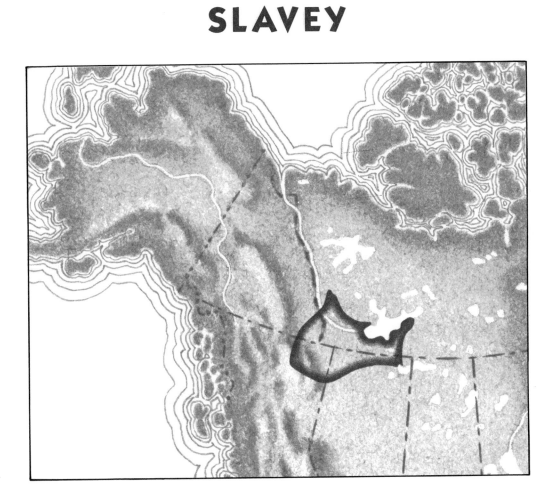

In this Slavey story, the animals get together and
wisely outwit the bear mother in order
to return summer to the world.

THE LONG WINTER

Before the present state of the world was established and when there were as yet no men, a very long winter set in. The sun was never seen, the air was dark, and thick clouds always covered the sky and hung low down. It snowed continually. After this had lasted three years, all the animals were suffering very much from want of food and still more from want of heat. They became greatly alarmed. A grand council was held, which beasts, birds, and fishes attended. It was noticed that no bears had been seen for three years and that they were the only creatures that did not go to the council.

The meeting decided that the great thing was to find out what had become of the heat, whose long absence was the cause of all their suffering, and, if possible, to bring it back again. In order to do this, they resolved that as many of them as possible, representing all classes, should go on a search expedition to the upper world, where they thought the heat was detained.

When the council broke up, they all set out, and after much traveling far and wide through the air, some of them were fortunate enough to find the door or opening to the upper regions, and they went in. Among those that were fortunate enough to get in were the lynx, the fox, the wolf, the wolverine, the mouse, the pike, and the dogfish.

After exploring for some time, they saw a lake and, beside it, a camp with a fire burning. On going to the camp, they found two young bears living there. They asked the cubs where their mother was and were told that she was off hunting. In the tepee, a number of full, round bags were hanging up. The visitors pointed to the first one and asked the young bears, "What is in this bag?"

"That," said they, "is where our mother keeps the rain."

"And what is in this one?" pointing to the second bag.

"That," they answered, "is the wind."

"And this one?"

"That is where Mother keeps the fog."

"And what may be in this next one?"

"Oh, we cannot let you know that," said the cubs, "for our mother told us it was a great secret, and if we tell, she will be very angry and will cuff our heads when she returns."

"Oh, don't be afraid," said the fox. "She will never know that you told us."

Then the cubs answered, "That is the bag where she keeps the heat."

The visitors had found out what they wanted, and they all went down to the tepee to hold a consultation. It was decided to retire to a distance, as the old bear might return at any time. But first they advised the young bears to keep a lookout for any deer that might come to the opposite shore.

It was resolved that the lynx should go around to the other side of the lake, turn into a deer, and show himself so as to attract the attention of the young bears. Meantime, the mouse was to go into the mother bear's canoe and gnaw a deep cut in the handle of her paddle, close to the blade. The others were all to conceal themselves near the old bear's tepee. When one of the little bears saw the supposed buck across the lake, he cried out, "Mother, Mother! Look at the deer on the opposite shore."

The old bear immediately jumped into her canoe and paddled toward it. The deer walked leisurely along the beach, pretending not to see the canoe so as to tempt the bear to paddle up close to him. Then all at once, he doubled about and ran the opposite way. The bear hastened to turn her canoe by a few powerful strokes, throwing her whole weight on the paddle, which broke suddenly where the mouse had gnawed it; the bear, falling at the same time on the side of the canoe, upset herself into the water.

The other animals were watching the hunt from the opposite side, and as soon as they saw the bear floundering in the water, they ran into the tepee, pulled down the bag containing the heat, and tugged it, one at a time, through the air toward the opening to the lower world from which they had come.

They ran as fast as they could, but the bag was very large and none of them was able to keep up the pace very long. Whenever one became tired out, another would take the bag, and so they all hurried along at a rapid rate, for they knew that the bear would soon get ashore and return to her tepee and that when she discovered her loss, she would quickly follow them.

Sure enough, she was soon in hot pursuit and had almost overtaken them before they reached the opening to the underworld. By this time, the stronger animals were all exhausted, and now the dogfish took the bag, pulled it along a good way, and, finally, the pike caught it up. He managed to get it through the hole just as the bear was upon the party. Everyone of them passed safely through at the same time, and the moment the bag was within the underworld, all the animals seized it and tore it open.

The heat rushed out and spread at once to all parts of the world and quickly thawed the vast accumulation of ice and snow. Its rapid melting flooded the earth, and the water rose until it threatened to drown all the animals that had survived the long winter. Many of them saved their lives by climbing up a particularly big tree that was much taller than any of the others in the woods. There was also a high mountain that others reached and were saved.

The poor beasts now cried loudly for someone to remove the water, and a great creature, something like a fish, appeared and drank it until he became as large as a mountain.

So the dry land returned, and as summer had come again, the trees, bushes, and flowers that had been covered by the ice leaved out once more; from that time until now, the world has always been just as we see it at the present day.

EASTERN WOODLAND CULTURE AREA

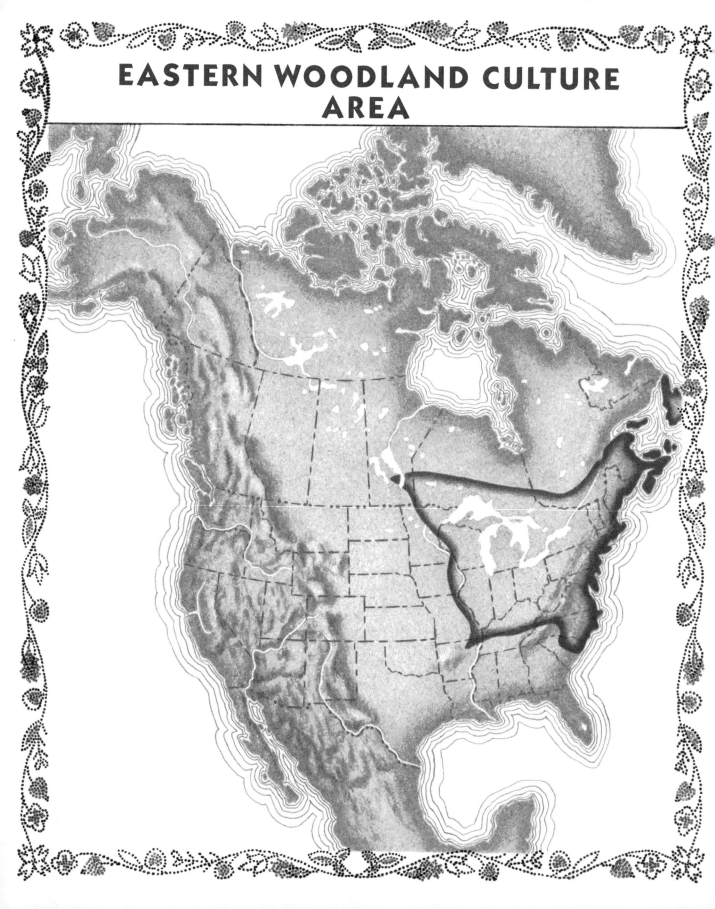

The Eastern Woodland culture area extends from the eastern edges of New Brunswick and Nova Scotia west to the Mississippi River, and from the area just north of the Great Lakes to the Carolinas and Ohio river drainage on the south. Tribes in this large area survived by a number of means. Some were primarily hunters of deer, bear, and wild fowl; others were fishermen, while yet others were mainly farmers who raised corn, beans, and squash. Some combined all of these economic endeavors. In the east, dwellings consisted of bark-covered longhouses with barrel-shaped roofs which were gathered into villages surrounded by sturdy stockades. Wigwams made of pole frames covered with mats, bark, or hides were used throughout the area. There was a strong concept of a "Master of Life" or a "Supreme Being." Dreams, shamans, secret societies, and curing ceremonies also occupied important places in the religious lives of the people.

PASSAMAQUODDY

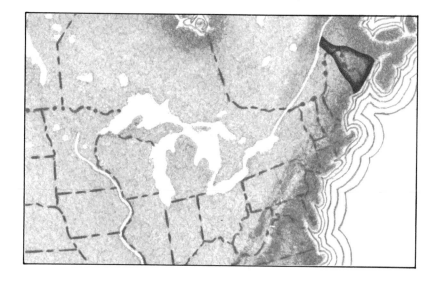

One myth of the Passamaquoddy tells about Kechi

Niwaskw, the good spirit. He lived on an island in the Atlantic Ocean and created

the first man and woman out of stone. However, the deity was

not satisfied with them, so he destroyed them and created two

others out of wood. All Indians are descended from them.

Opposed to Kechi Niwaskw was Machi Niwaskw,

who was an evil and powerful demon, much feared by the Passamaquoddy.

In "The Partridge's Wife," Mitchihess, the Partridge, hides

his dwarf brother in a box to protect him from Machi Niwaskw,

the evil one. The story tells what happened to the Partridge's wife when

the demon worked his evil.

THE PARTRIDGE'S WIFE

There was once a hunter who lived in the woods. He had a brother who was so small that he kept him in a box, and when he went out, he closed it very carefully for fear that an evil spirit would get him.

One day, this hunter, returning, saw a very beautiful girl sitting on a rock by a river, making a moccasin. Being in a canoe, he paddled up softly and silently to capture her. Seeing him coming, she jumped into the water and disappeared. On returning to her mother, who lived downstream, she was told to go back to the hunter and be his wife. "For now," said the mother, "you belong to that man."

The hunter's name was Mitchihess, the Partridge. When she came to his lodge, he was not there, so she arranged everything for his return, making a bed of boughs. At night, he came back with one beaver. This he divided; he cooked one half for supper and set aside the other half. In the morning when she awoke, he was gone, and the other half of the beaver had also disappeared. That night, he returned with another beaver, and the same thing took place again. Then she decided to spy and find out what all this meant.

So she laid down, pretending to sleep, but kept one eye open. She saw that he quickly rose and cooked the half of the beaver and, taking a key, unlocked a box and took out a little red dwarf and fed him. The small creature ate the entire half bea-ver. After feeding the dwarf, Mitchihess washed him and combed his hair, which seemed to delight him. Replacing the elf, he locked him up again and lay down to sleep.

The next morning, when her husband had gone for the day, the wife looked for the key and, having found it, opened the box and called to the little fellow to come out. This he refused to do for a long time, though she promised to wash and comb him. She finally persuaded him. He peeped out, and she pulled him out of the box. She started to groom him but whenever she touched him, her hands became red. This did not bother her because she thought she would be able to wash it off whenever she wanted to, but, while she was combing him, a hideous devil entered the room, caught the elf, and ran away with him.

She was terribly frightened. Though she tried to wash her hands, the red stain remained. When her husband returned that night, he had no game. When he saw the red stain, he immediately knew what had happened. He then seized his bow to beat her. She ran down to the river and jumped in to escape death at his hands, even though she knew that she would drown, but as she fell into the water, she became a sheldrake duck; to this day, the marks of the red stain are to be seen on her feet and feathers.

SENECA

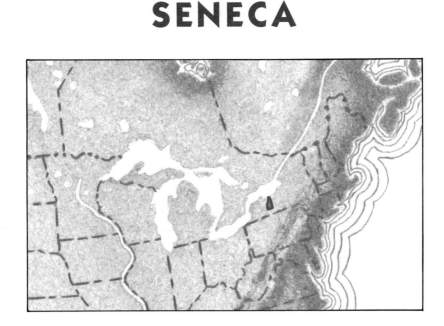

One of the Seneca creation myths tells how when only water existed on
earth, the water creatures got together to make land. Helldiver, the bird, swam down
deep below the water, picked up some mud, and brought it to the surface.
Turtle, floating on the water, became the base for an island; Beaver, sitting
on top of Turtle's shell, used his tail as a trowel and fastened the
mud to Turtle's back as the wet, sticky earth was brought up from below the
water. After a while, the land became as it is now, with all the creatures and
objects that exist on it. Long, long after the beginning of everything,
Turtle and Beaver met again. This next Seneca
tale relates how the two competed in a race in order to settle a territorial dispute.

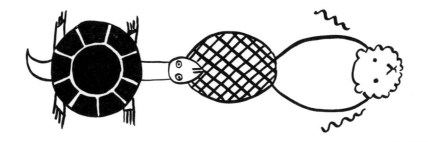

THE RACE OF THE TURTLE AND THE BEAVER

There was a turtle who lived in a deep hole in a stream. He lingered there, and it was a favorite spot for his fishing. On the shore, there was a swampy place where he hid himself when he left the stream.

One day, it grew very cold, and Turtle felt very sleepy. He looked around for a soft spot in the mud and found one beneath some tall, sheltering rushes. "Here I will sleep," said he. So saying this, he slept.

When he opened his eyes, there was a vast expanse of water over his head. Everything had changed, and all the rushes had vanished. He threw off the mud blanket that covered him and ambled out on the floor of his resting place. "Iik," he exclaimed. "Something has happened. Some magician has taken liberties with my home." Then he swam to the surface of the water.

Instead of the little stream with its neighboring swamp, he saw a big lake. As far as he could see, there was a lake. He looked around and saw an island in the lake, and he swam to it. It was covered with sticks, and, when he crawled upon it, there was a hollow sound within, which frightened Turtle and caused him to slip quietly off and conceal himself.

Soon he saw a dark form emerge from the water beneath the island, and the form rose to the surface.

Craftily, Turtle raised his head and called, "Who are you?" Then he submerged quickly.

There was a whistling answer, a slap of the water, and a voice said, "I am Beaver. Who are you?"

"So that is the case," thought Turtle. "Someone has stolen my fishing place." He was very angry and swam to the shore, where he saw all kinds of branches broken up by cutting. Soon he heard someone say, "Get out of my way."

Turtle looked up and saw Beaver dragging a branch.

"One would think," said Turtle, "that it should be *I* who said 'Get out of my way'."

"Well, what right do you have to be here?" asked Beaver.

"This is my home," said Turtle. "I have lived here a long time."

"Ho! Ho! Ho!" laughed Beaver. "If this is your home, where is your house? Now I say this is my home, for there is my house." He pointed to the thing that Turtle had thought was an island.

"How did you get here?" asked Turtle.

"I came here and built a dam, made this lake, and now I have a house here."

"I came here long ago," said Turtle, "and built a fishing hole. My home is in the swamp. You, O Beaver, have no right to spoil my home. I am going to break down your dam and restore my home."

"Well," said Beaver, "that would not do us any good for I would build another and others of my tribe would catch you and gnaw your head off."

"How shall we settle this thing?" asked Turtle.

"We shall see who can stay underwater longest," said Turtle.

"No, that would be too easy for me," said Beaver. "I could sleep a year underwater. I was going to ask that as a test myself. I propose that we run a race."

Turtle was annoyed, for he did not want Beaver to win, so he did not insist on the underwater test. He was also crafty, so he said, "Whoever wins the race shall stay here; whoever loses shall leave. First, we shall have a trial race, and then the race will begin."

They came abreast in the water and started to swim. Soon Turtle called Beaver back. "Now we will begin again," said he, with a wicked gleam in his black, beady eyes.

As they were about to start, Turtle said, "I will pur-posely lag behind. When I pinch your tail, then we will both start swimming."

Soon Turtle bit Beaver's tail and both started swimming. Crafty Turtle hung onto Beaver and was dragged through the water until they were in sight of the shore. Then he bit harder than ever.

Beaver gave a big grunt and whistled. "So, you are there behind me? Well, I will win yet!"

Turtle bit again, this time harder than ever, making Beaver squeal with pain. "I'll fix you for this," he called and flipped his tail over his head. Turtle hung on, and when he felt himself over Beaver's head, he let go and continued to speed through the air like a flying squirrel. He landed far away upon the shore, way ahead of Beaver.

"I have won this race!" he called back defiantly. "You must go away from here; this is my fishing pond."

Thereupon, Beaver was greatly annoyed and swam away to nurse his sore tail. Turtle had outwit-ted him.

CHIPPEWA

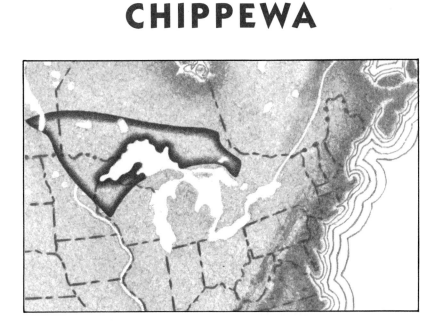

Eagles became objects of worship among the
Indians because of the birds' great size, strength, and their solitary and
mysterious nature. They were used for ceremonies and in art.
The wing bones were carved into whistles and used in religious rites or in warfare.
The feathers, particularly the white tail feathers with black tips,
were highly prized for their use in the making of ceremonial costumes.
Many of the stories told by the Chippewa were about contests
among groups of birds, animals, fish, and reptiles. In this next tale,
one such contest takes place. It tells how the eagle won
the contest because of its bravery and strength.

THE LINNET AND THE EAGLE

The birds met together, one day, to decide which could fly the highest. Some flew up very swiftly but soon got tired and were passed by others of stronger wing, but the eagle went up beyond them all and was ready to claim the victory when the gray linnet, a very small bird, flew from the eagle's back. It had perched there unnoticed and, being fresh and unexhausted, had succeeded in going the highest.

When the birds came down and met in council to award the prize, it was given to the eagle. Not only had he gone up nearer to the sun than any of the larger birds, but he had carried the linnet on his back.

Hence, the feathers of the eagle are prized as the most honorable marks for a warrior because the eagle is not only considered the bravest bird but it is also endowed with the strength to soar the highest.

WINNEBAGO

Born of the Winnebago god Earthmaker and a

human mother who dies in childbirth, Hare is raised by his grandmother, the

earth. In a long cycle of tales, Hare has many

adventures, several of which tell how he was chosen to become

the founder of an important ritual of the Winnebago,

the Medicine Rite. Hare kills all the evil

birds and all the evil spirits on land so they cannot

roam over it. At the end of the cycle, he becomes the transformer of the

world and the founder of the culture.

This story shows Hare

using his magic powers and explains why Hare has a slit nose.

HARE SLITS HIS NOSE WHILE VISITING

"Grandmother," said Hare one day, "I am going over to visit my uncles." "You may go," said she. So he left. On the way, he came to a large river, and he shouted, "Crabs, come here!" Immediately, a large number of crabs came over to him. He caught a large one and said, "Lend me your boat!" Then he skinned the crab and, turning up its tail for a sail, exclaimed, "Blow me across!" Then the wind changed and blew him across the river. So he sailed across in the shell of a crab, singing as he proceeded.

Finally he got to the other bank and, pulling his boat to one side, went on. Soon he came to a lodge, which he entered. Those within said, "Haho! Our grandson has come." Those within were people without bodies; they consisted only of heads.

All in turn stopped to greet him and said, "Our grandson must indeed be hungry." So they boiled something for him to eat. They boiled bear ribs with corn. This he ate, and he thought it delicious, and he ate a great deal of it. In eating, he used a knife that they had handed him. He would first bite a piece of meat and then cut it off. Suddenly, accidentally, he cut a slit in his nose. Blowing his nose, he yelled in pain.

"Our grandson has cut himself. Give him another knife." He was very pleased with the new knife they gave him and did not seem to mind the fact that he had cut himself.

Soon Hare went home. When he got home, his grandmother said, "Oh, my grandson has disfigured himself while visiting."

Ever since that time, even to the present day, whenever anyone goes visiting his uncles, they say he is going somewhere to slit his nose.

SOUTHEASTERN CULTURE AREA

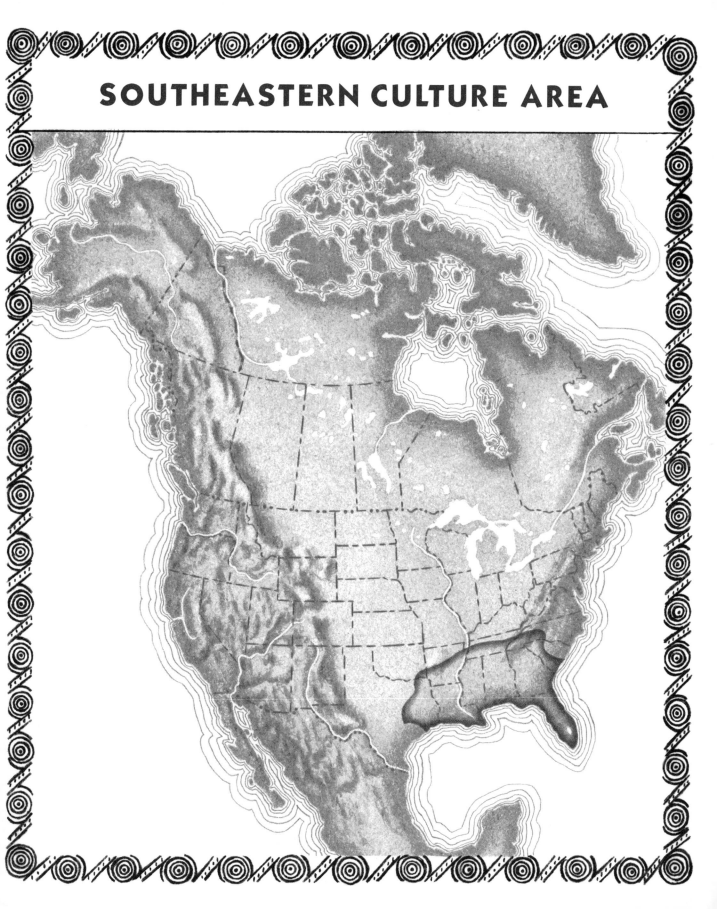

 The Southeastern culture area extends from the lower Atlantic coast to the lower Mississippi Valley, and from Tennessee to the Gulf of Mexico. The people usually lived in stockaded villages in houses, either round or rectangular, built of a framework of poles and covered with grass, a mud plaster, or thatch. In their nearby garden plots they raised corn, beans, melons, and also tobacco. These tribes   also hunted deer, bear, turkeys, and wildfowl; they fished and gathered nuts and berries, which grew profusely in the area. Harvest ceremonies and spiritual purification rituals were central to the religious system.

ALABAMA-COUSHATTA

Everything in existence, everything ever created,

had something of the supernatural attached to it, according to the Alabama-

Coushatta. Unexpected powers could be

granted to objects, such as birds, trees, people, animals, and

rocks. Sometimes these powers would be granted

for a special project, such as the creation of

the earth in this next story.

CRAWFISH, BUZZARD, AND THE CREATION OF THE EARTH

In the beginning, everything was covered by water. The only living things were a few small animals who occupied a raft floating on the water. Nothing else could be seen above the surface of the water.

One day, the animals decided that they wanted to make the land appear, so they called for a volunteer to make the attempt. Crawfish volunteered, and he dived off the raft. The water was so deep, however, that he was unable to reach the bottom of the great ocean.

Three days later, Crawfish again tried to reach the bottom, but again he failed. On the third try, he finally reached the bottom. Using his tail to scoop up the mud, he began building a great mud chimney. He worked rapidly, building it higher and higher, until the top of the mud chimney stuck up above the surface of the water. The mud began spreading to all sides, forming a great mass of soft earth.

The animals looked in all directions. They agreed that Crawfish had done a good job. However, they thought that the surface of the earth was too smooth, so Buzzard was sent out to shape the earth's surface.

Now Buzzard was a huge bird with long, powerful wings. He flew along just above the top of the soft earth, flapping his wings. When his wings swung down, they cut deep holes or valleys in the soft earth. When his wings swung up, they formed the hills and mountains. When Buzzard didn't flap his wings and just sailed along, he made the level country or plains.

And so the surface of the earth is made up of plains, valleys, and mountains.

CREEK

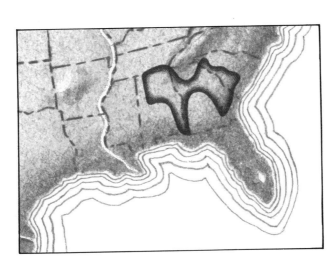

Part of a large group of native Americans called

Muskogean Indians, the Creek lived in Georgia and Alabama. Warlike and

highly organized socially, the Creek divided

themselves traditionally into two groups, the commoners

and the nobles.

Many of the Creek stories were about

Rabbit. In this tale, the Master provides him with

tasks so that the animal can find wisdom.

THE WISDOM OF RABBIT

Rabbit went to the Master and asked him for wisdom. He said, "I haven't much sense, and I want you to give me some more."

Then the Master gave Rabbit a sack and told him to fill it with small red ants. "Fill it," he said, "and I will teach you sense." The Master thought that if he didn't have any sense, he couldn't get even one ant into the sack.

Rabbit went to the anthill and said, "The Great Master has been saying that you could not fill this sack, but I said you could. What do you think about that?" They answered, "We will fill it," and, as they were very anxious to show that they could do so, they all went in, whereupon Rabbit tied it up and carried it to the Master. "Here it is," he said. "Now give me some knowledge."

The Master said, "There is a big rattlesnake over yonder. If you bring him here, I will give you some knowledge." He thought if Rabbit were really ignorant, he would not know what to do. Rabbit went off, cut a stick, and went to find the snake. Then he said to it, "The Master says you are not as long as this stick, but I say you are longer."

"I think I am longer. Measure me," said the snake. So Rabbit measured him by laying the stick beside the snake with its sharp end toward his head and, as he was doing so, ran the point into his head, killing him. He carried the snake back to the Master on the end of the stick.

Next the Master said, "There is an alligator over yonder in the lake. Bring him to me and I will give you knowledge." So Rabbit went to the lake and called out, "Halpata hadjo, halpata hadjo." The alligator came up in the middle of the lake and poked his head above the water. "What's the matter?" he asked. "An ox has been killed for the Master, and they want you to come and get timbers for a scaffold on which to roast it." So the alligator came out of the water and followed Rabbit. Before they had gone far, Rabbit turned around and struck him with a club. The alligator ran toward the lake, and although Rabbit pursued him, he got safely back into the water.

After that, Rabbit went off and lay down on the hillside in the sunshine for sometime. Then he went out and called to the alligator once more, "Halpata hadjo, halpata hadjo, halpata hadjo." The alligator came up in the middle of the lake as before and asked, "What's the matter?"

Rabbit, disguising his voice, replied, "Rabbit was sent here some time ago, and nothing has been seen of him, so they told me to come here to see what happened to him."

The alligator replied that someone had come to him before with such a story and had beaten him. "They thought he might have done something of the sort," said Rabbit, "for he is a mean, devilish kind of person. They told him to get you to bring the forked pieces for a scaffold on which to roast an ox and, as he didn't come back, they sent me to find out what happened."

Upon that, the alligator came out of the water again, and they set out. As they went along, Rabbit said, "That rabbit is very bad, and they ought not to have sent him. He has no sense. Did he beat you very badly?"

"He beat me a great deal, but he did not hit a dangerous place."

"If he had hit you in a dangerous place, would you have lived?"

"No, it would certainly have killed me."

"Where would you have to be hit in order for you to be hurt?"

"If I were struck across the hips, it would finish me."

Rabbit, having learned what he wanted to know, struck the alligator across the hips and laid him out dead. Then he picked him up and took him to the Master.

When the Master saw him with the dead alligator carried across his back, the Master said, "You have more sense now than I could ever give you."

HITCHITI

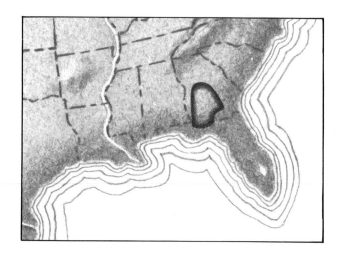

Among the Hitchiti, as with most Indian groups,

respect for elders was taught as an important part of the tribe's heritage.

This lesson is reinforced in the following

Hitchiti story.

THE WOLVES AND THE DOGS

The wolves used to go about with the dogs, but men made the dogs catch the young wolves and kill them. The wolves became angry, and a great number of them held a council. They said, "Our children are often killed. Let us gather the dogs together and kill them."

All agreed, so they started off and came howling about the house where the dogs lived. At the noise, the dogs howled back. Then the wolves howled in return and the dogs all assembled.

While they were talking to each other, the wolves said to them, "We are going to have a big chicken dinner at noon. All of you come and eat with us." The dogs answered, "All right." Then the wolves went back and dug a hole in the ground, and they waited until noon.

In the meantime, the dogs prepared to go to the feast. A very old dog wanted to go with them, but the others said to him, "You know you would not be able to travel around, so stay at home." He answered, "I can eat, too." While this dog was still at the house, the others all started off. Still, the old dog followed them. When they saw him coming, they said to one another, "That old dog ought to have stayed at home, but he is coming."

When they got to the place, a great number of the wolves were there, waiting for them and, when all were together, the wolves said, "Go into that big hole in the ground and sit down there." When the dogs got in, the wolves said to them, "Are you all here?" "An old one is coming," they answered, and they waited for him.

When the old male arrived, they said, "You go in there, too." So the old one went inside, and then one of four wolves sitting around the door to the hole in the ground stood up and said, "We have been looking for this chance to get you. You have killed all of our beautiful children, and now we are going to kill all of you." Another old wolf talked in this manner and lay down. Another stood up and said the same thing. Others spoke likewise.

Then the dogs cried and howled. The old dog to whom they had said, "You are fit for nothing and must remain in the house," the one that would not remain but went on, stood up and said, "I am the one who destroyed the children you said you lost, and I am getting pretty old."

He took out a wolf's tail that he was carrying with him and said, "Here is your tail, so kill me first." He shook the wolf tail at them, and when the old wolves saw it, they all jumped up and ran away. The dogs, not waiting for one another, jumped over the wall of the hole, got out, and ran off. After they had disappeared, the old dog walked around and went out.

When he got home, the dogs were already there, and he said, "You couldn't help yourselves, yet you said to me, 'Remain in the house; you are not able to travel around.' So you went along, and I set out and saved all of you. From this time on, rely on the old people when you go about. If one, older than the rest, advises you, trust him. Take his advice. All of you remember to do this. Before long, I shall be dead, but do not forget the advice I am giving you. Think, 'An old man who used to be with us saved our lives.'"

He advised them in this manner and not long afterward he died.

SEMINOLE

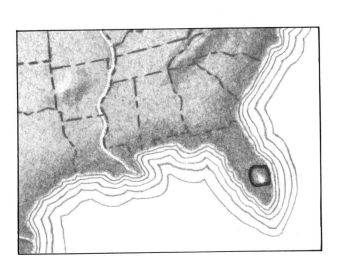

The Seminole tribe of Florida settled in the

Everglades area, a swampy, alligator-infested region to the south. Fond of

games, the Seminole tell how the alligator got the dent

on his nose during a contest between the animals

and the birds.

HOW THE ALLIGATOR'S NOSE WAS BROKEN

In the old days, all the animals decided to have a big ball game. The four-footed animals, with the alligator for their chief, challenged the birds, with the eagle at their head. Sides were chosen, the poles put up, the ground measured off, and the medicine men conjured the balls.

The day came, and they all met on the playing field. The animals ran around their poles, all painted and dressed up, while the birds flew and screamed around their poles.

At last, the ball was tossed into the air, and the game began. The alligator caught the ball as it came down and, grasping it in his teeth, ran toward the poles. The alligator's wife had run along with her husband and was shouting at the top of her voice, "Look at that alligator go! Just look at him!" while

all the animals cheered. The birds tried very hard to snatch the ball from the alligator, but finally, just as they were ready to give up, the eagle soared aloft and circled in the air until he was almost out of sight.

Then, like an arrow, he swooped to the earth and struck the alligator on the nose, denting it. When the eagle struck the alligator, the situation changed. The alligator's teeth opened on the ball, the turkey poked his head in among the teeth, pulled the ball out, and ran to the birds' poles, throwing the ball between them.

The birds won the game, and ever since that time, the alligator has had a sunken place on his nose where the eagle had struck it.

SOUTHWESTERN CULTURE AREA

The Southwestern culture area extends from western Texas on the east to the California border on the west, and from southern Utah and Colorado down into the Northern Mexican states of Sonora and Chihuahua. The people in this area were either agriculturalists who raised corn, beans, squash, and melons or else pastoralists who raised goats, sheep, cattle, and horses. Some combined both activities. Hunting and gathering were practiced by all groups. Warfare was commonly practiced by some of these groups, but not all of them. The Pueblo tribes lived in adobe apartment-house-type structures of connected rooms; the Navajos lived in hogans, which were six- or eight-sided log or wooden plank structures with domed roofs; and the Apaches, the third major group in this area, lived in tipis or in thatched wickiups that were circular and dome-shaped and were built of mesquite, cottonwood, or willow poles bound with yucca fiber and covered with brush and bear grass. The Pima Indians lived in round, flat-topped houses thatched with grass and covered with earth. Religions focused on agricultural themes and propitiation of game animals, as well as upon elaborate blessing and curing ceremonies.

JICARILLA APACHE

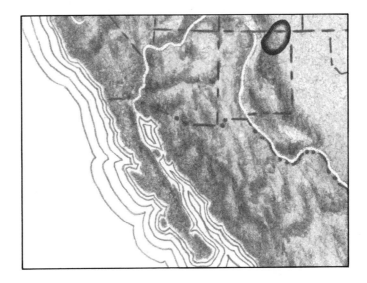

In this Jicarilla tale, Coyote, the cunning
trickster, is given the difficult task of obtaining fire from the
underground Firefly creatures.

ORIGIN OF FIRE

After the earth was formed, the Maker created Haschin to be his helper in the task of making the earth a good dwelling place for the people. Haschin made the animals, mountains, trees, and rivers, gave the people weapons and implements, and showed how they were to be used. When all were supplied with houses to live in and weapons with which to protect themselves and to kill game, he called Coyote, the mimic.

"Go to the Land of the Fireflies," he commanded, "and bring back their fire, for the people have no fire with which to cook their food."

Coyote started and found the Land of the Fireflies. These beings lived at the bottom of a deep, deep hole—an enormous cave in the solid rock. Its sides were smooth and straight, and Coyote did not know how to get down. He went to the edge of the pit and found Little Tree growing there.

"Help me down to the Land of the Fireflies," he said. So Little Tree sent its roots down, down, down, until they extended quite to the bottom, and Coyote descended. There he played with the little Firefly boys, romping about, running back and forth, pretending to be thinking of nothing but their amusement, for the Fireflies guarded their fire carefully and would let no one touch it.

Coyote had tied a tuft of cedar bark onto the tip of his tail. Suddenly, he dashed through the great fire that always burned in the center of the village and was off before the Firefly people knew what he had done. When they discovered that he had stolen some of the fire, they set out in pursuit, but Coyote was very swift of foot and reached the wall of the pit far ahead of them.

"Little Tree, help me out!" he called.

Little Tree drew its roots up, up, up, while Coyote held on and was drawn safely out of the hole. Then he ran quickly about among the people, lighting the piles of wood they had prepared, until every family was supplied with fire.

NAVAJO

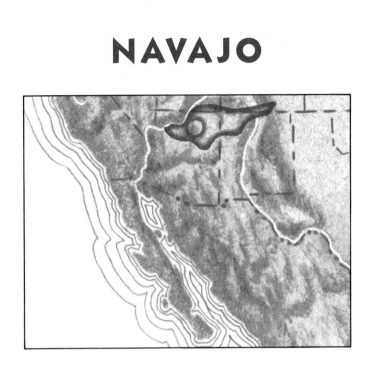

In this Navajo tale, Coyote joins his people
as they leave the fourth world and settle in the fifth world.

THE FLOOD

The Holy Ones made the First People from two perfect ears of corn, one white and one yellow. The white ear became First Man, and the yellow ear First Woman.

After First Man and First Woman were made, there soon were people all over the land. They began to make many farms, and everything was going along in a good way when a strange thing happened. They say that Coyote caused it to happen. Coyote and Badger had been born just after First Man and First Woman had been made, and Coyote was always visiting around and poking his long nose into things around the houses and farms.

One day he saw two little girls of The People (the Navajo) swimming across the river with their mother. Suddenly he saw these two little girls disappear under the waters. Coyote thought that the Water Monster had pulled the girls under the river, and he ran to tell everyone what had happened. The People looked everywhere, but it was not until the Holy Ones came to help them that they knew the little ones were safe in the home of the Water Monster under the waters. He had taken them down there so that they could become playmates for his own two little girls.

For three days and three nights The People searched for them. When the fourth morning came, they heard the call of the gods coming nearer and nearer, and then White Body and Blue Body appeared carrying large bowls of blue and white shell.

Placing these bowls on the surface of the river, they caused them to spin around and around and, gradually, to make a hole down through the water. They told a man and a woman to descend through this passage, and as these two did so, Coyote followed right along behind them.

Under the waters, they found a large and beautiful house of four rooms. The room in the east was made of dark whirling waters. The room in the south was of very blue, shining waters. In the west the room was of yellow sunset waters, and that in the north of all kinds of colored waters, changing and mixing together. This was the home of Tieholtsodi, the ruler of the waters.

The man and woman of The People went through the rooms looking for the two little girls. Coyote followed right behind them because he wanted to see how things were for himself. He followed them into the eastern room, but there was no one there. He followed them into the southern and western rooms, but they were empty. Finally in the northern room they all saw the Water Monster sitting playing with his own two little daughters and the little girls of The People.

The man and woman seized the two little girls and went back with them to the upper world. While they were doing this, Coyote picked up the two little water babies and hid them under his fur robe. Since he never took his robe off, even when he was sleeping, no one noticed anything as he came out of the waters. He was always skulking around anyway, so no one paid any attention to him.

But the next morning very strange things began to take place. The People were frightened to see that the sky was dark with all kinds of birds and squirrels flying and leaping into the camps. Also they saw herds of deer and antelope streaming past from east to west.

For three days there were flocks of turkeys and hawks and hummingbirds and bats flying over the farms. When the morning of the fourth day came, The People saw a gleaming white line on the eastern horizon, and they sent out messengers to see what this thing was. When they found that it was a flood of white, foaming water approaching them, they did not know what to do. There was water everywhere, the messengers said, water that was very deep and moving along very fast. The People felt helpless and could not decide what to do. The Kisani, the Pueblo people, joined them, and they wept and moaned all through the night.

When the dawn light came in the east, they saw that the waters were as high as mountains and encircling the whole horizon. The People packed up all their belongings and climbed to the top of the highest mountain. But as they climbed, the waters whirled around the base of the mountain and rose higher and higher. Then two of the Squirrel People planted the seeds of a juniper and a piñon tree, and The People had hope as they saw two tall trees grow higher and higher. But after a time, the trees began to branch out and to stop growing.

Then two of the Weasel People began to plant a pine and a spruce tree, and The People again hoped as they saw these trees grow faster and faster into the sky. But soon these trees began to branch out and to grow to small points at their tops, and then The People lost all hope. Just at this moment of their greatest need, as the waters were surging

higher and higher, two men were seen walking up the side of the mountain.

One was older than the other, for he had grey hair. The younger man walked in front of the older man, and as they ascended the mountain The People watched, but no one said a word. The two men sat down on the top of the mountain, facing east. The younger man told The People to move away and not to watch what his father and he were doing. From under his shirt, the old man took out many little buckskin bags which contained earth from all the mountains of the world. He spread this earth into a mound and planted thirty-two seeds in it.

When The People were told to return, they saw the roots of little reeds growing down into the earth of the mountain, and soon all the roots joined together and became a great reed which swayed gently as it grew toward the sky. There was a hole in its eastern side, and as the reed grew and grew, The People crowded into this entrance. When they were all safely inside, the hole was closed, and it was just in time.

Coyote was the first one inside the reed and Turkey was the last. His tail feathers were caught in the foam on the rising waters, and they have remained white even to this day, and the voice of the surging and foaming waters seemed to say, "Yin, Yin, Yin."

As the reed grew toward the sky, it began to sway back and forth, and The People were afraid. But Black Body drew a deep breath which he blew into a thick, dark cloud at the top of the reed, and this held it steady. When the reed touched the sky, they sent out the great Hawk to see if he could find a hole in the sky. He scratched and scratched with his claws, and finally disappeared from their sight.

When he returned, he told them that he had seen a faint light, but he had not been able to fly through to it. Then he sent out the Locust messenger, and when he returned, he told them he had

113

come out on a little island in the middle of a lake. He had seen four white birds which were either cranes or swans, and they had challenged his right to be in the new world. By this time, First Man had called on all of the digging animals to make a larger hole in the sky. The trail of Locust was too small for all The People. So Lynx, Bear, Badger, and Coyote clawed their way through and made a good path. Badger got his feet stuck in the black mud, and that is the reason his feet are black to this day.

First Man and First Woman led the way out of the reed onto the surface of the new world. It seemed to stretch out flat to the horizon. But they had the earth from the mountains of the fourth world with them, and they decided to make seven mountains in the new world with the earth.

The Holy Ones had come into the reeds with them, and all was beautiful in the new place which they named the fifth world, which is our present world.

ACOMA

The Acoma live in adobe and stone buildings on a

rock mesa in New Mexico.

Their settlement, or "pueblo," is considered

to be the oldest continuously inhabited place in the United States.

In the following story, the Acoma tell why the

tip of the fox's tail is white.

FOX GETS BACK HER FUR

Once there was a fox that fell asleep. She lived in a mouse town. The chief of the mice peeped out of his hole, saw the fox sleeping, and immediately went out and told the other mice what he had seen. They called a meeting, and the chief of the mice said, "Let us bite off all her fur. It will make a good bed for us."

So while the fox was asleep, they began to bite off her fur and put it aside. They had nearly finished biting off her fur and were just finishing the tail when one mouse bit a little too hard. The fox woke up, became angry, and killed many of the mice. The rest scurried into their holes.

Then the fox began to think about how she could get her fur back. Every once in a while, a mouse would peep out of a hole, and the fox would kill it. The chief of the mice then said, "Let us be careful from now on. Let us not stick our heads out, otherwise there will be none of us left."

The fox thought and thought about getting her fur back when she finally thought of using pitch. Far to the north, she found a little piñon tree full of sticky pitch, which she took and prepared into a paste. She then spread it all over her body.

Then she went back to the mouse village where her fur was. She took the fur, spread it on a smooth rock, and then rolled all over it. When she got up, her fur was again thick and long. The only difference was that the tip of her tail was now white. That was where the mouse bit too hard.

PIMA

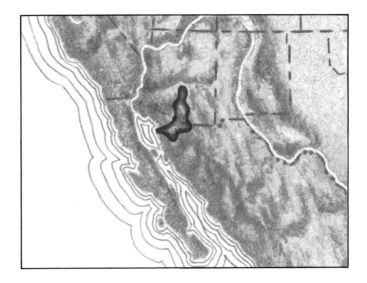

The Pima tribal historians were selected from
among those who showed an aptitude for remembering the stories and
traditions of their people. Boys were regularly
sent to these historians so that they could learn to carry on the
oral tradition. Many of these tales were about the
struggles of the Pima against the
demons, savage enemies, and gods that they
believed were ever-present.
In this last story, Roadrunner becomes a hero
in an encounter with Lightning God.

THE LEGEND OF THE ROADRUNNER

Long ago, when the world was new, Thadai, the Roadrunner, had beautiful, long plumage.

One day, when the Indians returned from the hunt, they discovered their fire had died down; only the gray ashes remained. The Indians asked Roadrunner to run to Lightning God, the keeper of the fire, and ask him for one of his fire sticks.

Roadrunner, being a good fellow, agreed and started at once for the mountain home of Lightning God. His strong legs helped him to "fold up the earth," and soon he reached his destination.

"What brings you here?" asked Lightning God.

"The Indians badly need fire."

"No!" Lightning God angrily retorted.

Roadrunner realized it was useless to ask again, so the first chance he had, he snatched one of the fire sticks from the blazing fire. Hastily placing it across his back and curling his tail over it, he scampered away.

Lightning God grabbed some flaming arrows and began shooting at Roadrunner. At the same moment, Roadrunner saw an arroyo and scurried into it, escaping the arrows. The beautiful plumes on his head were burnt off, leaving only a small tuft. His back was singed so that it became a brownish color, and his eyes turned red from the smoke.

Roadrunner successfully brought the fire stick to the Indians. When the squaws saw his tired, red eyes and his short, stiff, bushy head, they loudly wailed, "Shoik, shoik, shoik" ("Poor Bird"). Roadrunner was touched by their display of love and wailed, "Poi, poi, poi."

Ever since then, the Roadrunner has made his home in the chaparral. Whenever he finds a fat lizard, he cheerfully chants, "Thra, thra, thra!" When the Indians hear his chant, they smile gratefully, remembering what Roadrunner did for them.

"Nihancan's Feast of Beaver" by George A. Dorsey and Alfred L. Kroeber, *Traditions of the Arapaho,* Chicago: Field Columbian Museum, 1903, pp. 57-58.

"How the Seasons Came" by James L. Long, *The Assiniboines,* Norman: Univ. of Oklahoma Press, 1961, pp. 3-7.

"Spider's Revenge" ["The Adventures of Spider"] by Edward S. Curtis, *The North American Indian,* Cambridge, Mass.: The University Press, 1909, v. 5, pp. 134-136.

"Blood Clot" by Richard Erdoes and Alfonso Ortiz, *American Indian Myths and Legends,* New York: Pantheon Books, pp. 8-11.

"The Great Monster and the Great Flood" ["The Deluge"] by Edward S. Curtis, *The North American Indian,* Norwood, Mass.: Plimpton Press, 1911, v. 7, pp. 146-147.

"Coyote Kills a Giant" by Louisa McDermott, *Journal of American Folk-Lore,* v. XIV, 1901, pp. 242-243.

"The Wren" in "Folk-Tales of Salishan and Sahaptin Tribes" by James A. Tait (Franz Boas, ed.), *Memoirs of the American Folk-Lore Society,* Lancaster, Pa.: 1917, p. 118.

"The First Dawn" ["Blue Jay's Theft of Dawn"] by Cora DuBois and Dorothy Demetracopoulou, "Wintu Myths," *California University Publications in American Archaeology and Ethnology,* Berkeley: 1931, v. 28, pp. 300-301.

"Earth Namer and the Creation" by Roland B. Dixon, "Maidu Myths," *Bulletin of the American Museum of Natural History,* New York: 1902-1907, v. XVII, pp. 39-42, adapted by Robert E. McDowell and Edward Lavitt.

"The Origin of Fire" by Stephen Powers, "Karok Fables," *Contributions to North American Ethnology,* Washington DC: Government Printing Office, 1877, pp. 38-39.

"The Great Spirit and the Grizzlies" by Joaquin Miller, *Life Amongst the Modocs,* Hartford: American Publishing Co., 1874, pp. 264-276, adapted by Edward Lavitt.

"Beaver and Porcupine" by John R. Swanton, "Tlingit Myths and Texts," *Bureau of American Ethnology Bulletin 39,* Washington DC: Government Printing Office, 1909, p. 220.

"The Animal People Hold a Medicine Chant" by Edward S. Curtis, *The North American Indian,* Norwood, Mass.: Plimpton Press, 1911, v. 8, pp. 124-126.

"Red-Headed Woodpecker and the Thunderbirds" by Edward Sapir and Morris Swadesh, *Nootka Texts,* Philadelphia: University of Pennsylvania —Linguistic Society of America, 1939, pp. 51-55, adapted by Edward Lavitt.

"Raven Lights the World" by James Deans, "Tales from the Totems of the Hidery," Oscar Lovell Triggs, ed., Chicago: *Archives of the International Folk-Lore Association,* 1899, p. 25.

"Spider Comes to Earth" by Edward S. Curtis, *The North American Indian,* Norwood, Mass.: Plimpton Press, 1930, v. 20, pp. 85-86.

"The Owl and the Raven" by H. Rink and F. Boas, "Eskimo Tales and Songs," *Journal of American Folk-Lore,* 1894, v. 7, p. 49.

"When the Ravens Could Speak" by Knud Rasmussen, *Eskimo Folk-Tales,* W. Worster, trans., London: Glydendal Pub., 1921, p. 67.

"How Squirrels Came to Make Many Holes" by Edward S. Curtis, *The North American Indian,* Norwood, Mass.: Plimpton Press, 1930, v. 20, p. 224.

"Origin of Death and the Seasons" by Diamond Jenness, "Myths of the Carrier Indians of British Columbia," *Journal of American Folk-Lore,* 1934, v. 47, p. 249.

"White Bear and Black Bear" by James Mackintosh Bell, "The Fireside Stories of the Chippwyans [sic]," *Journal of American Folk-Lore,* 1903, v. XVI, p. 79.

"Wolverine the Thief" ["Wolverine and Wolf"] by James A. Teit, "Kaska Tales," *Journal of American Folk-Lore,* 1917, v. XXX, p. 471.

"The Long Winter" by Robert Bell, "Legends of the Slavey Indians of the Mackenzie River," *Journal of American Folk-Lore,* 1901, v. XIV, pp. 26-28.

"The Partridge's Wife" ["How One of the Partridge's Wives . . ."] by Charles G. Leland, *The Algonquin Legends of New England,* Boston: Houghton Mifflin, 1884, pp. 300-302.

"The Race of the Turtle and the Beaver" by Arthur C. Parker, *Seneca Myths and Folk-Tales,* Buffalo N.Y.: 1923, Buffalo Historical Society. pp. 309-311.

"The Linnet and Eagle" by Henry Rowe Schoolcraft, *Algic Researches,* New York: Harpers, 1839, v. II, p. 216.

"Hare Slits His Nose While Visiting" by Paul Radin, "Winnebago Hero Cycles: A Study in Aboriginal Literature," *Indiana University Publications in Anthropology and Linguistics,* 1948, Memoir I, pp. 100-101.

"Crawfish, Buzzard, and the Creation of the Earth" ["The Creation of the Earth"] by Howard N. Martin, in "Folk-Tales of the Alabama-Coushatta Indians," in *Mexican Border Ballads and Other Lore* by Mody C. Boatwright, ed., Austin: 1946, Texas Folk-Lore Society, pp. 65-66.

The following three stories are from "Myths of the Southeastern Indians" by John R. Swanton, *Bureau of American Ethnology,* Bulletin 88, Washington D.C.: 1929: "The Wisdom of Rabbit" ["The Tasks of Rabbit"], pp. 58-59; "The Wolves and the Dogs", pp. 100-101; "How the Alligator's Nose Was Broken", pp. 22-23.

"Origin of Fire" by Edward S. Curtis, *The North American Indian,* Cambridge Mass.: The University Press, 1907, v. I, p. 69.

"The Flood" by Margaret Schevill Link, *The Pollen Path: A Collection of Navajo Myths,* Stanford University Press, 1956, pp. 11-14.

"Fox Gets Back Her Fur" by Aurelio M. Espinosa, "Pueblo Indian Folk Tales," *Journal of American Folk-Lore,* 1936, v. 49, pp. 72-73.

"Legend of the Roadrunner" by Anna Shaw, *Pima Indian Legends,* University of Arizona, 1970, pp. 95-96.

INDEX